# An Illustrated History of Martial Arts in America

## 1900 to Present

### BY EMIL FARKAS

Photos of Bruce Lee used with express permission of Linda Lee Caldwell and Concord Moon LP.
ALL RIGHTS RESERVED.

*Book Layout:*
Tosha Lord

*Assistant Graphics:*
Colin Arnold, Derek Arnold, Brett Bailey, Rob Johnson,
Angel Lemus, and Tracy Warrener

ISBN #1-897307-90-X

© **Copyright 2007 Rising Sun Productions**

**Rising Sun Productions**
15805 Chase Street,
North Hills, CA 91343-6303
Tel. (818) 891-1133
www.risingsunproductions.net

An Illustrated History Of Martial Arts In America – 1900 to Present

# CONTRIBUTORS

1. **Caylor Adkins**: American karate pioneer and instructor.
2. **Yoshiaki Ajari**: American karate pioneer, Wado-ryu karate master.
3. **George Anderson**: American Martial Arts administrator, instructor, and international karate referee.
4. **Mike Anderson**: Co-founder of "Full Contact Karate", and martial arts promoter.
5. **Lou Angel**: American karate pioneer and Goju-Ryu karate expert.
6. **Jim Arvanitis**: Founder of "Modern Pankration".
7. **Aaron Banks**: American karate pioneer, and promoter of "Oriental World of Self-Defense".
8. **Jerry Beasley**: Karate instructor, author, and founder of the "Karate College".
9. **Bill Bly**: Founder of "American Samurai Magazine".
10. **Mitchell Bobrow**: American karate champion, president, and founder of "Otomix".
11. **Mel Bruno**: American Judo Pioneer
12. **Rob Calasanti**: President of NAPMA, author, and speaker.
13. **Art Camacho**: Martial Arts film director.
14. **Sid Campbell**: American karate pioneer, Shorin-ryu karate and kobudo expert.
15. **Ralph Castro**: American Kenpo Master.
16. **Larry Carnahan**: American karate champion, and president of the "North American Sport Karate Association".
17. **Nick Cerio**: American karate pioneer, and Kenpo expert.
18. **Mike Chat**: Founder of "Xtreme Martial Arts".
19. **Bill Clark**: Well-known Taekwondo instructor, speaker, and leading member of the "ATA".
20. **Joe Corley**: American karate pioneer, founder of the "Battle of Atlanta".
21. **Ray Dalke**: Shotokan champion and instructor.
22. **Fred Degerburg**: Famous martial arts instructor, and promoter.
23. **Fumio Demura**: Former All Japan champion, and Shito-ryu karate master.
24. **George Dillman**: American karate pioneer, and U.S. karate champion.
25. **William Dometrich**: American karate pioneer, Chito-ryu karate expert.
26. **Dr. Terrance Webster Doyle**: Famous martial arts author, and instructor.
27. **Isaac Florentine**: Hollywood director.
28. **Leo Fong**: American kung-fu promoter, author, and film producer.
29. **George Foon**: Former art director of "Inside Kung-fu Magazine" and publisher.
30. **Brian Frost**: Koeikan karate expert, and instructor.
31. **Kenneth Funakoshi**: Shotokan karate expert, and champion.
32. **Royce Gracie**: Introduced Brazilian Jujitsu to the U.S., and founded the "UFC".
33. **John Graden**: Founder of "NAPMA".
34. **Jim Harrison**: American karate pioneer, and U.S. champion.
35. **Bong Soo Han**: Hapkido master, and martial arts fight choreographer.
36. **Morio Higaonna**: Okinawan Goju-ryu karate master.
37. **Stephen Hayes**: American Ninjitsu expert.
38. **Joe Hyams**: American author, and former student of Bruce Lee.
39. **Dan Ivan**: American karate pioneer, and author.
40. **Jimmy Jones**: American karate champion, instructor, and promoter.
41. **Pat Johnson**: American karate champion, and leading Hollywood fight coordinator.
42. **Roy Kurban**: American karate champion, and promoter.
43. **Ed Kaloudis**: American karate pioneer, and Koeikan karate expert.
44. **Ken Knudson**: American karate champion.
45. **Phil Koeppel**: American karate pioneer, and one of the top members of the "USKA".
46. **Takayuki Kubota**: Gosoku-ryu karate master.
47. **Gene Le Bell**: American judo champion, author, and Hollywood stuntman.
48. **Linda Lee Caldwell**: Bruce Lee's wife.
49. **Shannon Lee Keasler**: Bruce Lee's daughter.
50. **Steve Le Velle**: Martial arts instructor, and leading martial arts business expert and speaker.
51. **Cliff Lenderman**: Martial arts instructor, and actor.
52. **Joe Lewis**: American karate, and kickboxing champion
53. **Ernest Lieb**: Famous American karate instructor, and founder of the "American Karate Association".
54. **Andrew Linick**: American karate pioneer, and author.
55. **Ron Marchini**: American karate champion, and Rembukan karate expert.
56. **Chuck Merriman**: American karate pioneer, and Okinawan Goju-ryu karate expert.
57. **Ken Min**: Martial arts pioneer, coach, and physical education director at U.C. Berkley.
58. **Anthony Mirakian**: American karate pioneer, and Okinawan Goju-ryu karate expert.
59. **Hidy Ochiai**: American karate pioneer, and Washin-ryu karate master.
60. **Ed Parker**: Founder of "American Kenpo".
61. **John Pellegrini**: Founder of "Combat Hapkido".
62. **Ernie Reyes**: Famous Taekwondo champion, instructor, and coach.
63. **Jhoon Rhee**: Father of Taekwondo in America.
64. **Robin Rielly**: American karate pioneer, author, and Shotokan expert.
65. **Don Rodriguez**: American karate instructor, promoter, coach of the "John Paul Mitchell Karate".
66. **Cynthia Rothrock**: American karate champion, and motion picture actress.
67. **Frank Sanchez**: Founder of the "Sokeship Council".
68. **Hal Sharp**: American Judo pioneer, and author.
69. **Frank Silverman**: Martial arts instructor, martial arts business expert, and speaker.
70. **Jeff Smith**: American karate champion, and instructor.
71. **Allan Steen**: American karate pioneer, promoter, and champion.
72. **Alex Sternberg**: American karate champion, coach, and Shotokan karate expert.
73. **Mary Townsley**: American martial arts photo journalist.
74. **Robert Trias**: father of Karate in America.
75. **Peter Urban**: American karate pioneer, founder of "USA Goju".
76. **Ron Van Clief**: American karate champion, and actor
77. **Carlos Velez II**: Famous American martial arts journalist.
78. **Keith Vitali**: American karate champion.
79. **Bernie Weiss**: Past president of "ATMA".
80. **David Weiss**: Author, son of Al Weiss, and founder of "Official Karate".
81. **Curtis Wong**: Founder of "Inside Kung-fu Magazine".
82. **Pat Worley**: American karate champion, and well known instructor.
83. **Keith Yates**: American Taekwondo instructor, author, and journalist.
84. **Kiyoshi Yamazaki**: Ryobukai karate expert, and Kobudo master.
85. **Bob Wall**: Owner of "World Black Belt.com".
86. **Don Warrener**: President of "Rising Sun Productions".

## EMIL FARKAS
### AUTHOR, MARTIAL ARTS HISTORIAN

Hungarian-born American martial arts instructor, author and fight-coordinator, Emil Farkas started his martial arts career while still a youngster, and before age 20 he had earned his black belt in both Judo and Karate. Today, he is one of America's most respected senseis and is internationally recognized as an authority on the martial arts. He holds a 7th degree Black Belt in Karate, 4th degree Black Belt in Judo and a 4th degree Black Belt in Ju-Jutsu. He is also a noted expert in realistic street combat, having worked as a bodyguard for many years.

Farkas, who came to the United States in 1965, was one of the first martial artists to use his expertise to choreograph realistic fight sequences for television and films. In 1970, while still heavily involved in the film industry, he opened his dojo, the Beverly Hills Karate Academy, which is still in the same location today.

Over the years, Farkas has taught martial arts to many of Hollywood's leading stars, and today, he specializes in teaching private lessons at his own dojo or in private residences. Among his students are numerous celebrities, as well as top business executives.

Since 1970, Farkas has written articles for every major martial arts magazine and has authored a number of books, including **The Complete Martial Arts Catalogue** (Simon & Schuster), **Fight Back: A Woman's Guide to Self-Defense** (Holt, Reinhart, Winston), **The Overlook Martial Arts Dictionary** (Viking), **Training & Fighting Skills with World Champion Benny Urquidez** (Unique Publications), **Who's Who in the Martial Arts** with Bob Wall, and the most authoritative book on the arts ever written, **The Martial Arts Encyclopedia**, which sold nearly 150,000 copies.

He co-wrote the original screenplay for **Force 5** and wrote and co-produced the feature film **Vendetta**. Farkas has a set of six instructional tapes on **Combat Shotokan** and a set of five tapes on **Combat Ju-Jutsu**. He has also released a video on **Cane Fighting** and one on **Realistic Street Combat**. He is now working on his newest video, **Simple Self-defense for Children**.

In 2000, Farkas and Benny "The Jet" Urquidez founded the Los Angeles Film Fighting Institute, which was one of the first schools of its type in the U.S. to teach martial artists the intricacies of stunt work. Farkas has been featured on the cover of over a dozen martial arts magazines in the United States and abroad, and has had dozens of articles written on him and his system of "Combat Shotokan". Currently, he is working on a major reference book, **The Martial Arts Book of Knowledge** and has just finished his first novel with a martial arts flare, **Going for Silver**.

In addition to his martial arts skills, Farkas is also an accomplished magician and is a member of the world famous Magic Castle in Hollywood.

## DON WARRENER
### PUBLISHER

Don Warrener began his karate training March 15, 1966, in Hamilton, Canada, under Benny Allen, who also taught Wally Slocki, Teddy Martin and Tony Faceti.

He was promoted to shodan (1st degree black belt) in 1968 by Benny Allen and the legendary Richard Kim of San Francisco, California. He won the Canadian Championship in 1968 and, in 1971, won the Eastern Canadian Championships. In 1973, he broke the "Guinness World Book of Records" record for brick breaking when he broke 3,744 bricks in 4 hours and 40 minutes.

In 1978, he was introduced by his sensei, Richard Kim to Gogen "The Cat" Yamaguchi, who asked him to represent the Goju Kai in Canada. He refused, as his loyalty remained with Richard Kim. Although he did return to Tokyo on several occasions for training at the dojo of the "The Cat".

During the late 1970s, he started the "Voice Of The Martial Arts Magazine" and "Masters Publication", now run by Annette Hellingrath. He also started to develop a system of teaching large numbers of students and school marketing which eventually developed into over 9,000 students by the late 1980s, and opened over 32 professional schools – all in Canada – and selling 105 franchises. He, in fact, was the first person in the world to teach martial arts business seminars.

In 1985, he began the lengthy process of restoring a national monument and, with the aid of his students, restored the historic Hamilton Custom House (20,000 sq. feet) which was originally commissioned by Queen Victoria. He was presented with the Heritage Award of Canada in 1991 for his efforts and contributions by the Federal Government. The building was scheduled to become a college for martial arts instructors but, due to circumstances beyond his control, it was eventually turned over to the Provincial Government as a museum, which it is today.

In 1993, he became vice president of the World Karate Organization and eventually held the largest International tournament ever in Canada, with over 27 countries and 1,200 participants – with over 700 Black Belts.

In 1997, he started to compete again and won the European and Pan American Championships in both forms and weapons in the Masters Division of the WKO.

He presently runs Rising Sun Productions with his partner Isaac Florentine, a well known martial artist and Hollywood action film director. Their library is now over 650 titles and they were responsible for the release of Elvis Presley's pet karate project, "The New Gladiators". They undoubtedly have the largest collection of unseen historical martial arts footage in the world, including names like Kano, Funakoshi, Elvis Presley, and Bruce Lee.

He continues to teach seminars around the world – in England, for friends Jon Jepson and Jim Wilson; in Brazil, for Antonio Flavia Testa and Marco Fierra; in Scotland, for Robert Smith; and, for his senior students in Canada: Phil McColl, Conroy Copeland, Tosha Lord, Tom Burtnik, David Turkoski and Vic Granic.

He has written over 250 articles for virtually every martial arts magazine in the world. He has also written six books in total and co-authored another six. He has just completed his most recent book, "20th Century Samurai", which is the life and legend of Richard "Biggie" Kim.

He was recently promoted to 8th dan by the ButokuDo Organization, with members in Canada, USA, England, Brazil and Scotland.

# BOB WALL
## PRODUCER

Bob Wall, in costume from the set of **Enter the Dragon**.

Bob Wall was born in San Jose, California. He then moved to Los Angeles, trained with the Great Gene LeBell and began studying Okinawa-te where he met Joe Lewis in 1964. Bob Wall is a Black Belt under Gene LeBell, became Joe Lewis' first Black Belt in 1967 and has a Black Belt from Chuck Norris.

They formed a partnership and opened the famed "Sherman Oaks Karate Studio," training ground for many super stars such as Bruce Lee, Chuck Norris, Mike Stone, Pat Burleson, Jim Harrison, Benny Urquidez, Steve McQueen, Priscilla Presley, Jack Palance, Johnny Desmond, Freddie Prinze, Brian Keith and many more.

In 1967, Joe Lewis sold his interest to the legendary Chuck Norris, and he and Bob Wall built the most successful chain of karate studios in United States history. In 1973, Wall and Norris sold out to a conglomerate, and Norris went on to become a super star actor and Wall a real estate magnate.

In 1975, Wall authored the first "Who's Who in the Martial Arts" with over 130 male and female greats of the martial arts, a revised second edition in 2003 and third in 2006.

Bob Wall took 1st or 2nd in every major karate championship from 1965 to 1972 including the World Championship, the Internationals, the United States Championship, the National Championships, the Tournament of Champions, and was a member of the legendary quintet of Chuck Norris, Mike Stone, Joe Lewis, Skipper Mullins, and Bob Wall in sweeping the world professional titles for 1970, 1971 and 1972.

He starred with his wife Lillian, in "Lawman Jeans" commercials, Hai Karate, and Black Belt cologne commercials with Chuck Norris and Mike Stone. He was a founding member with Chuck Norris of the "World Pro-Am Championships" and the "Four Seasons Championships." Wall has been featured on the front covers of many magazines including "Black Belt", "Fighting Stars", "Karate Revue", "Official Karate", "Karate", "Professional Karate", "Budo", "Inside Karate", " Karate Journal", "Fighter", "Karate Illustrated", "Karate News", "Action Karate", "Fighting Spirit", "Martial Arts", "Action Martial Arts", "World News", "Traditional Karate", "Budo Karate" and "Martial Arts Professional".

Bob Wall was voted into the "Professional Karate Hall of Fame" in 1975, listed in the "Who's Who of Karate" in 1980, the "Who's Who in California" in 1982/83, and also the "Who's Who in Business and Finance" in 1983/84. Wall was given the Texas Karate Hall of Fame in 1987, and the International Karate Hall of Fame award in 1988, was inducted into the "Martial Arts Museum Hall of Fame" in 1990, the Karate Black Belt Hall of Fame in 1991 and is featured on the first "Karate Trading Cards." Wall was also inducted into the USA International Karate Hall of Fame in 1995, American Martial Arts Hall of Fame in 1999, the Masters Hall of Fame in 2000, the GSKA Black Belt Hall of Fame in 2000 and received the Karate Team Fighter of the Century Award in 2001. He was also inducted in the Warrior/Gentleman Hall of Fame in 2001, the Action Martial Arts Hall of Fame in 2002, the Blue Grass Nationals Hall of Fame in 2003 and received the Living Legends Fighter Award in 2003. He received the Living Legends Pioneer Award in 2003 and was inducted into the Legend of Martial Arts Hall of Fame in 2004.

In January 2000 Bob Wall became a founding member and President/CEO of World Black Belt, Inc., a worldwide martial art community, which has the WBB MasterCard, Knockout Fitness Recovery Drink, the Kickbar (a great protein bar), the America in Defense program which contracted with American Airlines for World Black Belt and American In Defense cabin crew self defense program.

# FOREWORD

As a martial arts historian I had, for years, contemplated writing a pictorial book on the history of American martial arts. Over the years, I have been fortunate to have met and befriended many of the greats of the American martial arts world, from the masters to the pioneers and from the leading champions to the well-known instructors. These people were the ones responsible for the phenomenal growth of martial arts in this country and I wanted to pay homage to them. This book is the result of my tribute to all of them.

I began collecting photos for this book a number of years ago, but with a busy schedule, my progress was slow and I put the book on hold.

Then, suddenly, I noticed that some of the great martial arts legends were beginning to pass away and I realized that it was time to work on the book seriously. Now motivated, I dropped other projects and began a concerted effort at collecting the photos that I needed. The journey to the finished product was, at times, difficult. Priceless photos were often stored in weathered cardboard boxes in corners of dojos and homes. Many great martial artists who had passed away left few photos that could be found and often classic pictures were thrown away.

But, thanks to the hundreds of fellow martial artists who were willing to help, the project slowly began to take shape. People took the time to dig into those old boxes and finally sent me rare and invaluable photos that make this book so unique. After a few years, I felt I had a collection of pictures that would fully illustrate the history of martial arts in America; however, it was only because of the immense help of these contributors that this project became a reality.

Although this book contains only a fraction of the photos that exist, it's my hope that for today's generation and, perhaps for future generations, these photographs will reflect the history of martial arts in a country that was introduced to a centuries-old tradition only in the early 1900s.

As I continue my journey as a historian, please join me in finding and preserving important photographs and documents that will enlighten the next generation of martial artists about our unfolding history and timeless traditions.

Yours in the martial arts,
Emil Farkas

*This book is dedicated
to all those who have given tirelessly
to the advacement of Martial Arts in America.
~ Thank you.*

# Timeline

1903
• Yoshiaki Yamashita demonstrates judo for the first time in the U.S.

1904
• U.S. President Theodore Roosevelt starts studying judo with Yoshiaki Yamashita.

1907
• The first Kodokan judo school in the U.S. opens in Seattle.

1909
• Kali is introduced to the U.S. by Jack Santos.
• First judo dojo, the Shunyokan, opens in Hawaii.

1913
• Jigoro Kano visits Hawaii for the first time.

1920
• American Army officer Allan Corstorphin Smith publishes, *The Secrets of Ju-jitsu: A Complete Course in Self Defense*.
• Okinawan karate master Kentsu Yabu visits Hawaii and Los Angeles and demonstrates karate.

1929
• Henry Okazaki, Hawaiian martial arts instructor, publishes *The Science of Self-Defense for Girls and Women*.

1930
• Ark-Yuey Wong begins teaching kung-fu to Los Angeles-based Wong Wen-Sun Chinese Benevolent Association.
• Henry Okazaki establishes Danzan ryu ju-jutsu on Oahu, Hawaii.

1932
• Hawaiian Judo Yudanshakai (Black Belt Association) is founded.
• Shuji Mikami opens the first kendo school outside of Japan in Honolulu, Hawaii.

## 1933
- The first karate club to allow Caucasian membership is formed in the basement of Honolulu's First Methodist Church. Its instructors are Mutsu Zuiho and Kamesuke Higaonna.

## 1934
- Gojo-ryu karate master Chojun Miyagi visits Honolulu where he demonstrates and teaches karate.

## 1936
- Taoro Mori begins teaching kendo in Los Angeles.

## 1940
- The first intercollegiate judo competition takes place in Northern California between San Jose State and U.C. Berkeley.

## 1942
- James Mitose starts to teach ju-jitsu in Honolulu.

## 1944
- William K.S. Chow begins teaching martial arts classes at the Nuuahu YMCA in Honolulu.

## 1946
- Robert Trias establishes the first karate dojo in the continental United States, in Phoenix, Arizona.

## 1947
- Kajukenbo, the first eclectic martial art in the U.S., is created by five Hawaiian martial artists: Walter Choo, Joseph Holke, Frank Ordonez, Adriano Emperado and Clarence Chang.

## 1948
- Henry Stone of California introduces weight divisions to U.S. judo competition.
- The United States Karate Association is founded by Robert Trias. It is the first karate organization in the U.S.

## 1949
- The Amateur Athletic Union recognizes judo as an official sport.

## 1952
- Karate Master Mas Oyama tours the U.S. and introduces karate to the American masses for the first time.

## 1953
- The U.S. Judo Black Belt Federation is formed.
- Koichi Tohei introduces aikido to Hawaii.
- The first Collegiate Judo Tournament is held in Berkeley, California.
- The first national AAU Judo Championship is held in San Jose, California
- Mel Bruno, under the sponsorship of Strategic Air Command, organizes a tour by 10 leading Japanese martial arts experts, who demonstrate their skills at Air Force bases across the country. The arts include judo, karate and aikido.

## 1954
- Ed Parker begins teaching kenpo karate in Provo, Utah.
- The San Diego Judo Club introduces aikido to the continental United States.
- Ed Kaloudis introduces Koeikan karate on the U.S. East Coast.
- William Dometrich introduces chito-ryu karate to the U.S. in Covington, Kentucky.
- Bobby Lowe founds the first overseas branch of kyoku shinkai karate in Honolulu.

## 1955
- The first after-school judo program is started by George Wilson at Kent Washington's Kentridge High School.
- The first karate tournament in the U.S. is held by Robert Trias in Phoenix, Arizona.
- Shotokan karate is introduced to the U.S. by Tsutomu Oshima, who begins teaching in Los Angeles.

## 1956
- The first commercial karate dojo is opened in Honolulu by Carlton Shimomi. The style is shorin-ryu.
- Jerome Mackey introduces franchise martial arts to the U.S. when he opens a chain of judo clubs in New York City.
- Jhoon Rhee introduces taekwondo to the U.S. when he begins teaching in San Marcos, Texas.

• Ed Parker moves to Pasadena and opens his first West Coast dojo.

1957
• Matsubayashi shorin-ryu karate instructor Louis Kowloski of St. Louis opens the first karate school in the Midwest.
• Cecil Patterson a wado-ryu karate instructor becomes one of the first to teach karate in the South. He begins teaching in Tennessee.
• Gordon Doversola introduces Okinawa-te to the U.S. He begins teaching in Los Angeles.

1958
• George Mattson introduces uechi-ryu karate to the U.S. He begins teaching in Massachusetts and opens the first karate school in the New England States.
• Mas Tsuroka introduces chito-ryu karate to Canada. He begins teaching in Toronto.
• Tsutomu Oshima sponsors the first Nisei Week Karate Championships in Los Angeles. It is the first traditional karate tournament in the U.S.

1959
• Peter Urban introduces Japanese goju-ryu karate to the U.S. He begins teaching in Union City, New Jersey.
• Hiroshi Orito introduces Renbukai karate to the U.S. in New York City.
• Alan Lee introduces Shaolin kung-fu on the East Coast, in New York City.
• Bruce Lee comes to Seattle and begins teaching wing chun in a covered parking lot of a Blue Cross clinic.
• Hidetaka Nishiyama's and Richard C. Brown's book, *Karate: The Art of Empty Hand Fighting,* is published in the U.S. It becomes an all time classic.

1960
• Anthony Mirakian introduces Okinawan goju-ryu karate in the U.S. He begins teaching in Watertown, Massachusetts.
• Yoshiaki Ajari begins to teach wado-ryu karate in Hayward, California.
• Dr. Maung Gyi introduces bando in the U.S. and begins teaching in Washington, D.C.

• S. Henry Cho opens the first taekwondo school in New York City.
• Isshin-ryu karate instructor, Steve Armstrong, begins to teach in Tacoma, Washington.

1961
• *Black Belt Magazine* unveils its first issue. Its founders are Mito and Jim Uyehara.
• Rusty Glichman, a female judoka, defeats a male opponent in an AAU sanctioned judo competition and the AAU bans women from participating in judo competition. It took 10 years for the ban to be lifted.
• Gosen Yamaguchi (son of Gogen "The Cat" Yamaguchi) introduces goju kai karate in California, while attending college in San Francisco.
• Richard Kim introduces shorin-ryu karate to the U.S. when he begins to teach at the Chinese YMCA in San Francisco.
• Teruyuki Okazaki one of the JKA's top instructors, opens a dojo in Philadelphia where he begins teaching shotokan karate.
• Hidetaka Nishiyama, one of Japan's leading shotokan karate instructors moves to Los Angeles and founds the All American Karate Federation.
• John Pachivas begins teaching karate in Florida.
• Hidetaka Nishiyama promotes the first large traditional karate tournament in the U.S., The All America Karate Federation Championships, in Los Angeles.
• American television viewers see karate for the first time when Bruce Tegner demonstrates the art in an episode of the TV series, *The Detectives*.

1962
• John Leong introduces hung gar and tai chi chuan to Seattle, and includes many non-Chinese among his students.
• Chang Man-Che'eng publishes the first English language text of tai chi, *Tai Chi Ch'uan: A Simplified Method of Calisthenics for Health and Self-Defense.*
• Mas Oyama's Kyohushinkai Organization sponsors the first open tournament in the U.S., the Northwest American Karate Championships held in New York City.
• Al Weiss and Johnny Kuhl from New York produce *Combat Karate*, the first American magazine dealing exclusively with karate.

- Allen Steen opens the first karate school in Dallas.
- The first national collegiate judo championship is conduced at the U.S Air Force Academy in Colorado Springs.
- The National Collegiate Judo Association is founded.
- Gene LeBell defeats boxer Milo Savage in the first Boxer vs. Martial Artist contest - Salt Laske City, Utah.

1963
- Robert Trias and John Keehan produce the first national karate tournament in the U.S. It was held in Chicago.
- Chuck Norris opens his first dojo in Torrance, California, where he teaches Tang soo do.
- Uechi-ryu karate instructor George Mattson is the first American to author a book on traditional karate style, *The Way of Karate*.
- Burmese bando expert Maung Gyi introduces bando to the U.S. and founds the American Bando Association.

1964
- J. Pat Burleson wins the First National Karate Championship
- Angel Cabales of Stockton, California opens the first school that teaches the Filipino martial arts to non-Filipinos.
- Tsutomu Oshima begins teaching the first accredited college karate course in the U.S. at the California Institute of Technology in Pasadena, California.
- Sea Oh Choi introduces hapkido to the U.S. when he begins teaching in Los Angeles.
- Jhoon Rhee promotes the first National Karate Championships in Washington, D.C.
- Ed Parker promotes the first Long Beach International Karate Championships.
- Bruce Lee makes his first major public appearance when he demonstrates at the Long Beach International Karate Championships in California.
- Mike Stone wins International Karate Grand Championship

1965
- Shito-ryu karate is introduced to the U.S. by Fumio Demura, who begins teaching in Santa Ana, California.
- Pauline Short opens the first karate school for women located in Portland, Oregon.
- Television covers sport karate for the first time when they televise karate matches from Jhoon Rhee's second National Karate Championships.

1966
- Jim and Al Tracey begin to franchise karate schools all over the U.S., which was the first large-scale karate franchise operation in the U.S.
- Bruce Lee begins his role as Kato on the TV series *The Green Hornet*.
- The USA Goju organization is founded by karate sensei Peter Urban of New York.
- Joe Lewis and Bob Wall open Sherman Oaks Karate Dojo, first upscale martial arts school

1967
- Ninjas are introduced to the American public when the James Bond movie *You Only Live Twice* is released nationwide.
- In New York, Aaron Banks promotes the first karate team competition.
- Shorinji kempo is introduced to the U.S. by Hirokazu Yamamori.
- Bruce Lee names his system jeet kune do.
- Top ten ratings for karate competitors begin by *Black Belt Magazine*.
- John Keehan conducts the first bare knuckle full contact event in the U.S. in Chicago.
- Chuck Norris and Bob Wall create the first martial arts billing company, Martial Arts Acceptance.

1968
- Al Weiss begins publishing *Official Karate Magazine*, out of offices in Manhattan.
- Mito Uyehara publisher of *Black Belt Magazine* begins Black Belt Hall of Fame.
- The first professional karate tournament in the U.S. is promoted by Jim Harrison in Kansas City, Kansas.
- **The PKA founded by Chuck Norris, Bob Wall and Mike Stone.**

1969
- Mito Uyehara begins publishing *Karate Illustrated Magazine*.
- The American Tae Kwon Do Association is founded in Little Rock, Arkansas by Haeng Ung Lee.
- The U.S. Judo Association is formed.

1970
- Chuck Norris, Joe Lewis, Mike Stone, Bob Wall and Skipper Mullins win the first World Professional Karate team title.

• Joe Corley and Chris McLoughlin begin promoting the Battle of Atlanta Karate Championships.

1972
• The first martial arts T.V series in America, *Kung Fu,* begins to air on ABC.
• *Billy Jack* is the first American movie to feature the Korean art of hapkido, which is instrumental in beginning the martial arts boom that followed.
• Jhoon Rhee develops Safe-T-Equipment which revolutionizes American karate tournaments.
• AAU recognizes karate as an official sport.
• The American Collegiate Taekwondo Association is formed.

1973
• *Inside Kung-Fu Magazine* is founded by Curtis Wong in Los Angeles.
• *Enter the Dragon* is released and makes Bruce Lee a superstar.
• Mike Anderson's Top Ten Nationals in St. Louis begins semi-contact karate competition. Howard Jackson wins.

1974
• Wu Shu Troupe from China tours the U.S. for the first time.
• Amateur Athletic Union recognizes taekwondo as an official sport.
• General Choi Hong Hi moves to Toronto and the International Taekwondo Federation is now headquartered there.

1975
• Second World Professional Karate Championship is held in Los Angeles. Promoted by Mike Anderson, the event begins an era of full contact karate.
• Harold Long founds the International Goshinryu Karate Association, headquartered in Knoxville, Tennessee.
• An estimated 50 million views watch Jeff Smith and Karriem Allah compete in 11 round full contact karate event. The fight was a preliminary bout to the Muhammed Ali/Joe Frazier fight "Thrilla in Manila " with Bob Wall doing commentary.

• Hidetaka Nishiyama conducts the first International Amateur Karate Federation World Championships in Los Angeles.

1977
• Teruyuki Okazaki, based in Philadelphia, founds the International Shotokan Karate Federation.
• The North American Tae Kwon Do Union is founded.

1979
• Graciella Casillas becomes the world's first female full contact world companion.
• ESPN signs a deal with the Professional Karate Association for the right to broadcast full contact karate tournaments.

1980
• Curtis Wong begins a new magazine, *Kick Illustrated*.
• Stephen Hayes introduces togakure-ryu ninjutsu to the U.S. and the ninja craze in America begins.
• Chung Ding Sheng, grandmasters of shuai chiao tours America.

1982
• The martial arts video revolution begins when Joe Jennings founds Panther Video.

1987
• Mike Swain becomes the first American judoka to win a gold medal at the World Judo Championships.

1988
• Dana Hee and Arlene Limas become the first Americans to win Olympic taekwondo gold medals.

1989
• Billy Blanks' tae bo becomes the newest exercise fad in America.

1991
• Cardio kickboxing begins to become a popular form of aerobic exercise especially among women.

1993
• Ultimate Fighting Championships is founded.

- No holds barred fighting begins to gain popularity across the country.
- Due to the UFC, grappling begins to become widely practiced, especially Brazilian ju-jutsu.
- *Dragon: The Bruce Lee Story* is released in theatres.
- *Walker, Texas Ranger* begins on CBS starring Chuck Norris.

1994
- NAPMA is founded by John Graden.

1995
- Martial arts related websites are beginning to have a presence on the Internet.

1996
- Martial Arts Professional Magazine is launched by NAPMA.

1998
- K-1 comes to the U.S.

1999
- World Black Belt is founded by 53 amazing martial arts legends including Gene LeBell, Pat Burleson, Jim Harrison, Cung Le and General Choi Hong Hi.

2001
- The Martial Arts Industry Association (MAIA) is formed.
- Little Ninjas Program begins; promoted by NAPMA it launches the boom in the pre-school karate program.
- World Black Belt founders Lou Casamassa, David Krapes, Soloman Kaihewalu, Deanna Bivins and Bob Wall create AID, Aviation in Defense, and contract with Amercan Airlines to teach cabin crew self defense.
- Chuck Platten becomes Canadian Director of World Black Belt.

2004
- "Curse of the Dragon", a documentary about Bruce Lee, produced by Fred Weintraub.
- World Black Belt creates the ultimate anti-aging, anti-disease beverage: KO Fitness Recovery Drink.

2006
- Mixed Martial Arts becomes the new craze, with television embracing it, and the public getting behind it.

2007
- History Channel's Human Weapon exposes millions of viewers to the real martial arts from around the world.

# The 1900s

Ju-jutsu is the Oriental martial art that was practiced sparingly in the U.S. at the beginning of the century. In 1903, Yoshiaki Yamashita gave the first demonstration of Kodokan judo in Seattle and then moved to the East Coast where a few of Washington's and New York's elite trained under him. Among his students was president Theodore Roosevelt.

One or two judo dojos sprang up on the West Coast where a large number of Japanese resided, but across the country it was ju-jutsu that one could learn if an instructor could be found.

Only one or two books on the Japanese self-defense systems were published before 1910. and very few Americans had heard of ju-justsu or judo.

An Illustrated History Of Martial Arts In America – 1900 to Present

Ju jitsu was introduced to America in the early 1900s.

Shown here is early American ju-jitsu, often referred to as self defense tricks.

Below and at right are more self defense tricks.

Yoshiaki Yamashita was among the first judo instructors in the United States. A high-ranking black belt, he came to the United States in 1903 and among his students was President Theodore Roosevelt. Yamashita also taught judo at the U.S. Naval Academy.

The 1900s

Hawaii was the first place judo was practiced in the United States. Here a group of students are seen (circa 1902).
*Courtesy of Mel Bruno*

At left, the first English language book on judo, published in America in 1904

One of the earliest English language books on jiu-jitsu, it was published in 1905.

A signed photo to Y. Yamashita from President Theodore Roosevelt, his judo student. **President Roosevelt was a 3rd degree black belt in judo.**

The 1900s

A few women were studying judo as early as 1906, as these photos illustrate. Of these, most were relatively wealthy and participated in private lessons.

An Illustrated History Of Martial Arts In America – 1900 to Present

**Judo master Yamashita** (second from left) with his wife in Washington. President Roosevelt, who studied with Yamashita, had a judo dojo built in the White House during the early 1900s.

One of the earliest ads for jiu-jitsu training, around 1908.

*Courtesy of Mel Bruno*

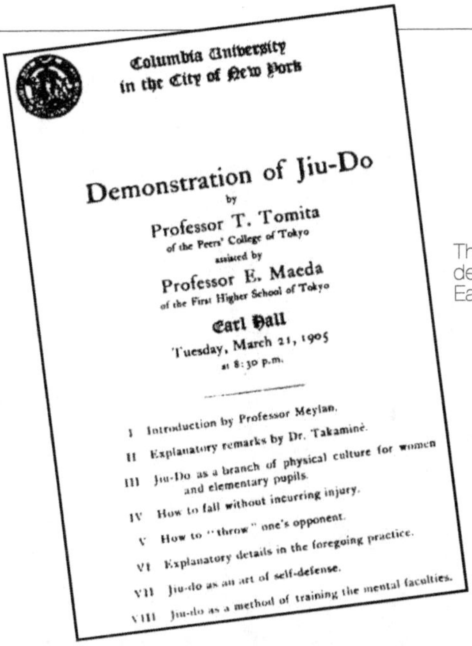

Columbia University
in the City of New York

Demonstration of Jiu-Do
by
Professor T. Tomita
of the Peers' College of Tokyo
assisted by
Professor E. Maeda
of the First Higher School of Tokyo

Earl Hall
Tuesday, March 21, 1905
at 8:30 p.m.

I Introduction by Professor Meylan.
II Explanatory remarks by Dr. Takaminé.
III Jiu-Do as a branch of physical culture for women and elementary pupils.
IV How to fall without incurring injury.
V How to "throw" one's opponent.
VI Explanatory details in the foregoing practice.
VII Jiu-do as an art of self-defense.
VIII Jiu-do as a method of training the mental faculties.

This was one of the first demonstrations of judo on the East Coast of the U.S.

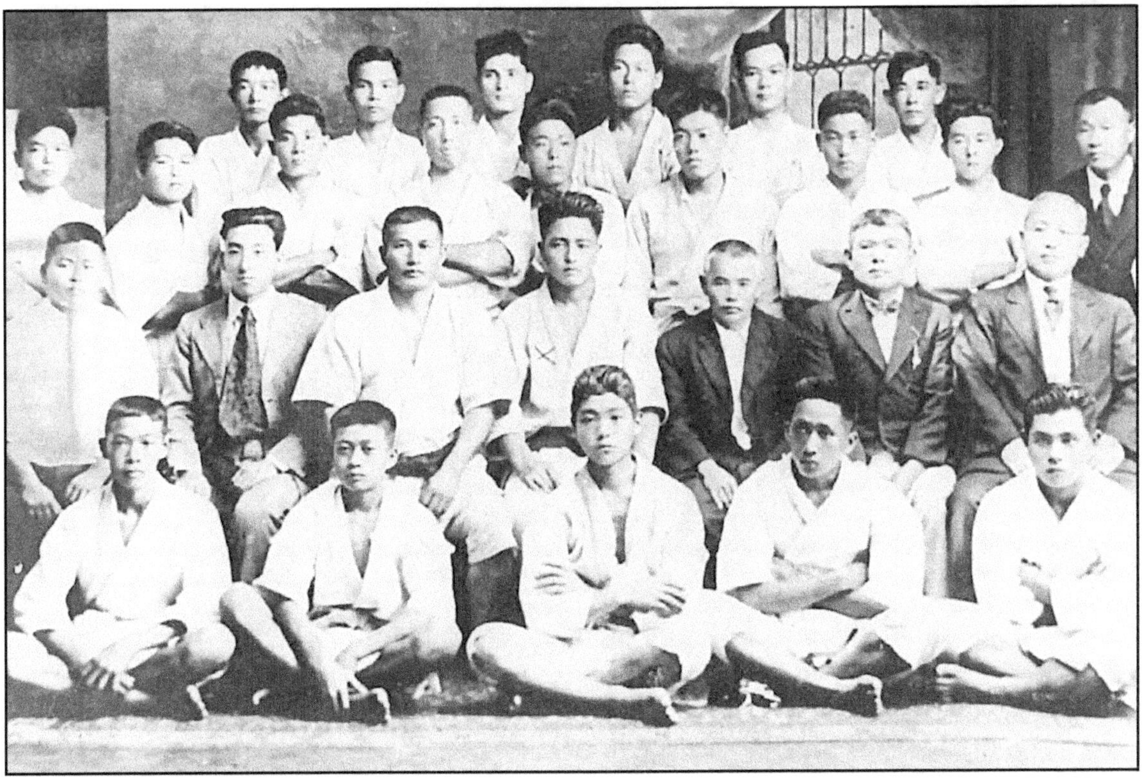

Members of a Hawaii judo dojo are seen here around 1909.

# The 1910s

By now, a few more Japanese judo instructors had come to the U.S. and few judo dojos could be found – especially in Hawaii and the Pacific Northwest.

With World War I, many of the U.S. soldiers were exposed to a few ju-jutsu techniques in their basic training, and now a number of ju-jutsu books began to appear. The public became more aware of the Oriental fighting arts. Most of those who trained were members of the upper class and most instruction was done privately.

The 1910s

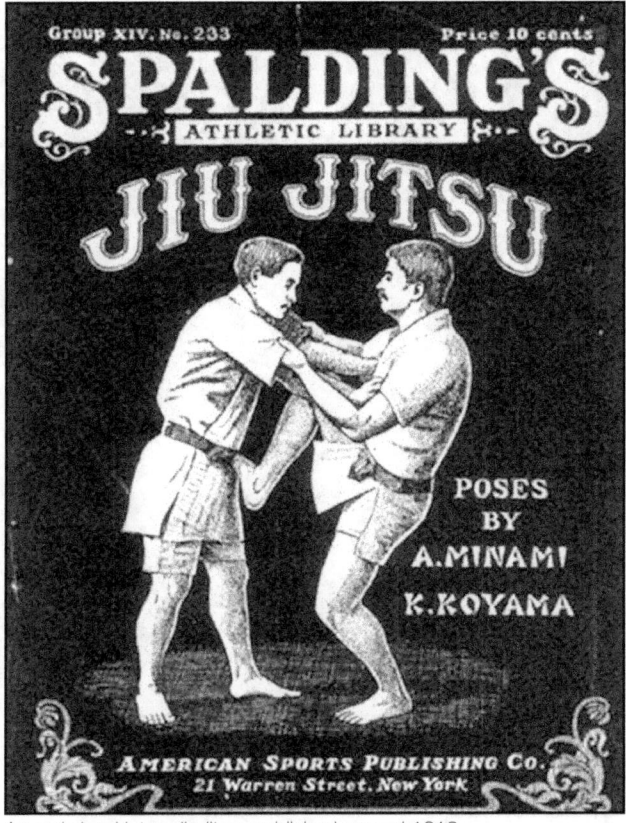

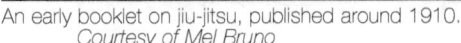
An early booklet on jiu-jitsu, published around 1910.
*Courtesy of Mel Bruno*

By the early 1900s a few women from upper class backgrounds were practicing the little known art of ju-jutsu for self-defense. This photo shows a New York woman in training in 1910.

By around 1915 a fair number of Americans were practicing judo.

One of the earliest judo clubs in Hawaii was the Shobu Kan Dojo. Seen here are some of its members in 1910.

An Illustrated History Of Martial Arts In America – 1900 to Present

One of the earliest judo clubs in the United States was the Shinyokai dojo in Hawaii. By 1911, as this photo shows, the school had a fair number of members. The head sensei was Kichimatsu Tanaha (seen here in a suit). Henry Okazaki, who later became one of Hawaii's leading senseis, is seen on the far right standing.

Two groups of American soldiers practicing ju-jitsu techniques around the end of World War I.

The 1910s

The Secrets of
JUJITSU
柔術

A
Complete Course
In
SELF DEFENSE

By
CAPTAIN ALLAN CORSTORPHIN SMITH, U. S. A.
Winner of the Black Belt, Japan, 1916.
Instructor of Hand-to-Hand Fighting,
THE INFANTRY SCHOOL,
Camp Benning, Columbus, Georgia
and at United States Training Camps and Cantonments,
1917 and 1918.

In Seven Books
Book 1

This book was actually published in 1917-1918 as seven booklets, each covering certain areas of this self-defense art.

It features rare photographs of uniformed soldiers training during the first World War era.

An early Hawaiian judo club in 1916.

An Illustrated History Of Martial Arts In America – 1900 to Present

# The 1920s

    Judo was gaining ground as more and more major cities opened dojos and both judo clubs and ju-jutsu clubs flourished, although there were still few and found mostly in the bigger cities.
    With crime on the increase, people sought out self-defense training and a few Americans were getting good at these arts.
    A few magazine articles about judo appeared, and a lot more books were now being published on judo, ju-jitsu and self-defense.
    A number of instructors began giving public demonstrations of judo and, in Hawaii, karate was introduced, but not widely practiced.

# The 1920s

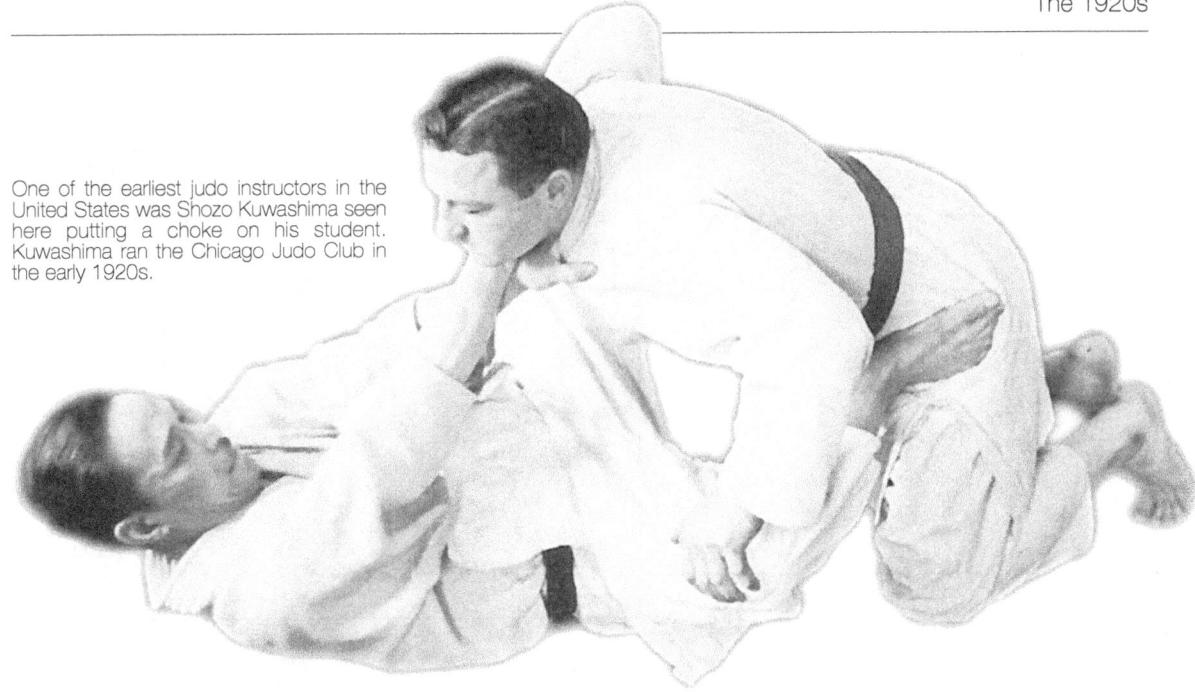

One of the earliest judo instructors in the United States was Shozo Kuwashima seen here putting a choke on his student. Kuwashima ran the Chicago Judo Club in the early 1920s.

Jigaro Kano visited the Biltmore Hotel in downtown Los Angeles in the 1920s to discuss judo in the Olympics. He can be seen 8th from the left, along with many other American and Olympic judo dignitaries.

Ju-jutsu classes were readily available in Hawaii as early as the 1920s. Here is a typical dojo from that era.

Kendo was one of the first martial arts practiced in America, but mostly by the Japanese who immigrated here during the early 1900s. Since the 1960s, kendo dojos have sprung up in all large American cities, but it is still practiced mostly by Japanese.

An Illustrated History Of Martial Arts In America – 1900 to Present

The Shunyo Kan club in Hawaii was one of the earliest judo dojos in North America. Founded in 1909 by Teshima Shigemi and Kaneshige Naomatsu, it is still in existence. Shown here are some of the dojos members in 1926.

Famous Okinawan karate master Yabu Kentsu (in suit) on a visit to Hawaii in 1927, where he demonstrated and taught karate.

By the late 1920s Seishiro Okazaki (seated) was a well-established instructor in Hawaii. He was teaching jiu jitsu and doing massage.

World Champion boxer Jack Dempsey, left, with Setsuzo Ota in 1926.

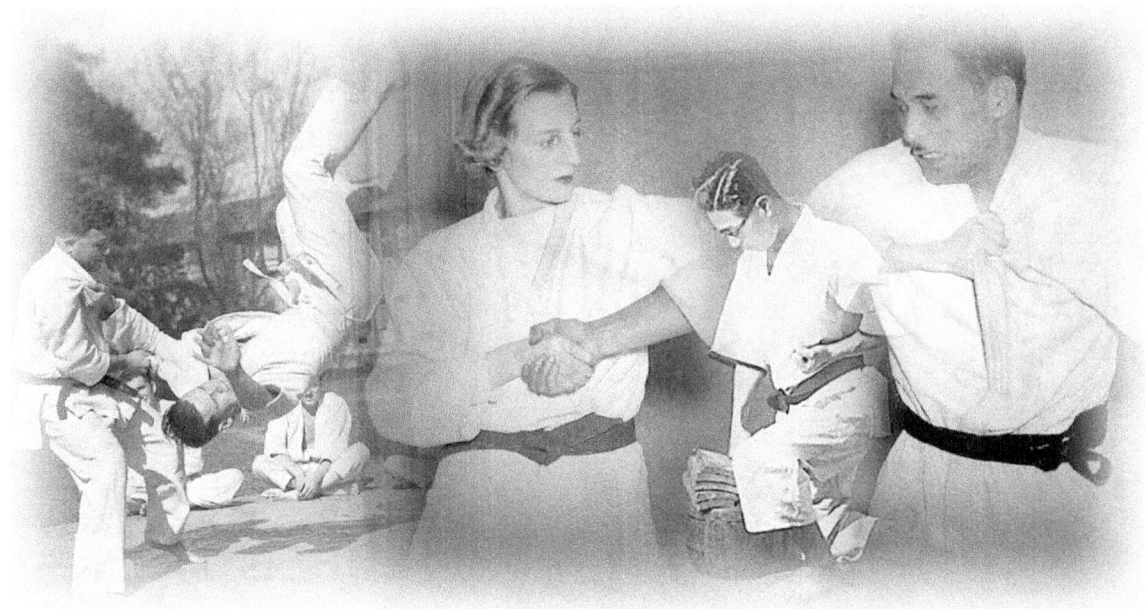

# The 1930s

Judo was coming to be more talked about and newspapers often had articles on the strange self-defense art where a small man could overcome a bigger opponent by scientific means. A number of mainstream magazines ran lengthy articles on judo and ju-jutsu and a few Americans had reached black belt level and were teaching the arts.

In the late 1930s some West Coast colleges began to teach judo and soon competition between schools was beginning to take place.

Books on the subject were now numerous and the public was becoming aware of what judo was. Judo dojos were now to be found in most major cities, and YMCAs and athletic clubs began to offer judo classes.

In some Chinese communities, especially on the West Coast, kung-fu was secretly practiced, and in many Japanese communities kendo was gaining popularity.

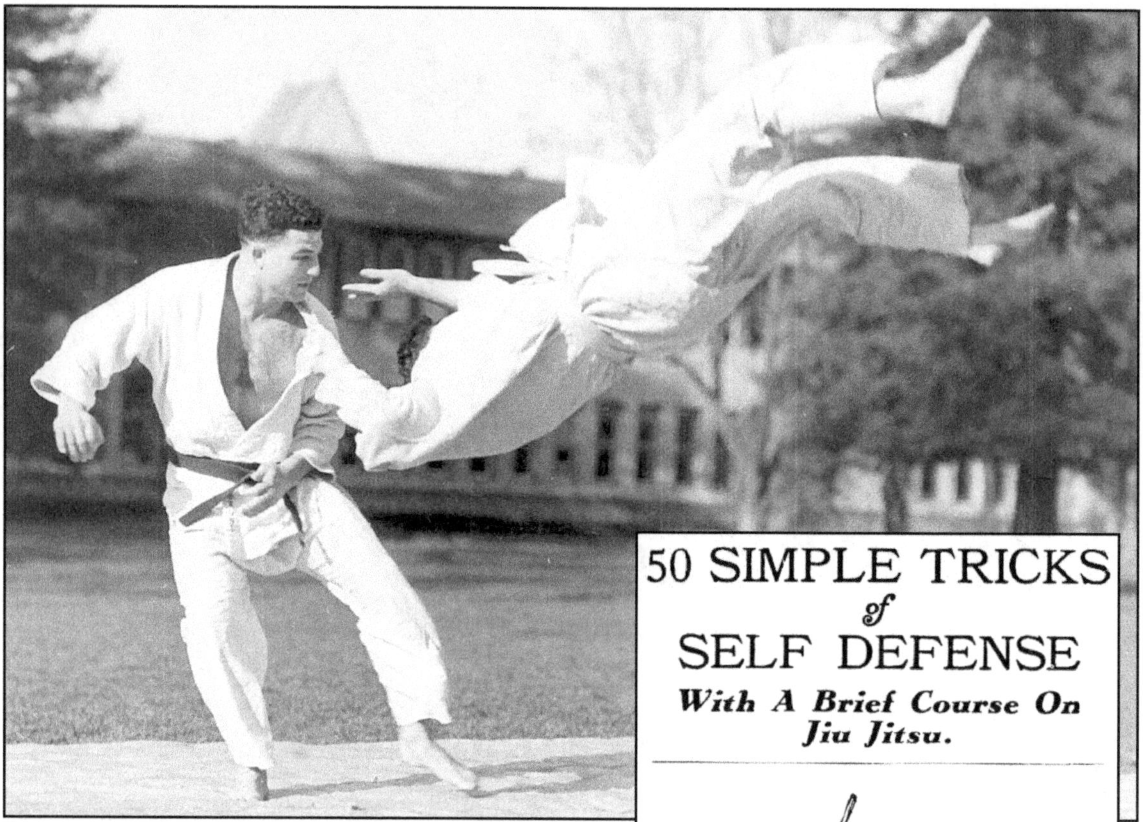

Judo pioneer Mel Bruno (left) is seen here in the early 1930s.
*Courtesy of Mel Bruno*

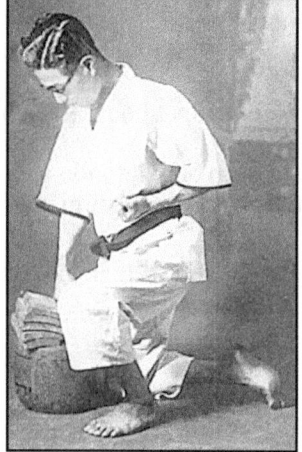

Karate Master Kamesuke Higashionna in early 1930s Hawaii.

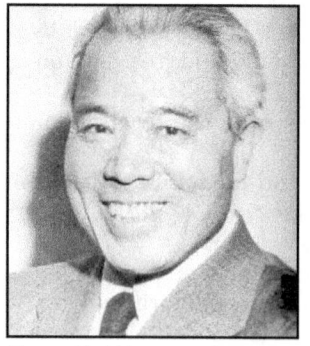

George Yoshida was a Japanese-American judo pioneer who ran the most famous East Coast Judo dojo, the New York Dojo, established in the 1920s. Yoshida was instrumental in forming the New York Yudanshakai in 1961 and became its honorary president.

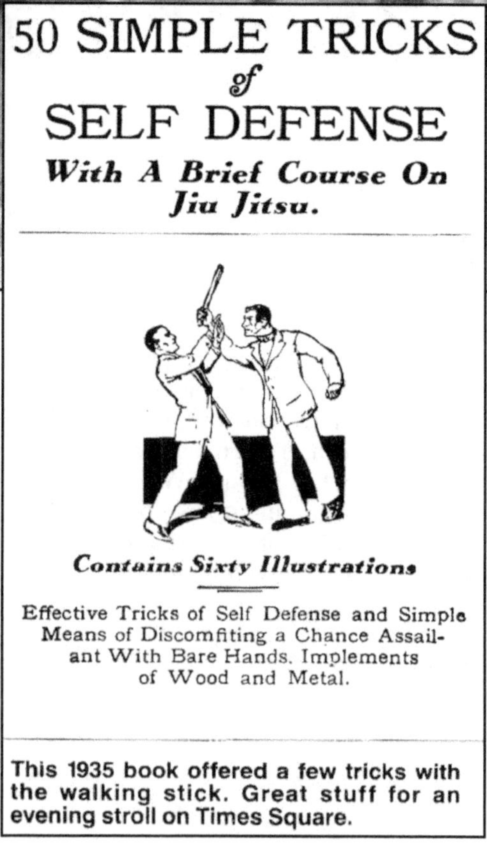

50 SIMPLE TRICKS
of
SELF DEFENSE
***With A Brief Course On Jiu Jitsu.***

***Contains Sixty Illustrations***

Effective Tricks of Self Defense and Simple Means of Discomfiting a Chance Assailant With Bare Hands. Implements of Wood and Metal.

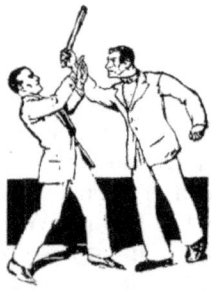

**This 1935 book offered a few tricks with the walking stick. Great stuff for an evening stroll on Times Square.**

An early book on Jiu-Jitsu published in 1935.

## The 1930s

By the early 1930s a few of the women training in ju-jutsu were getting very proficient, as seen here in a rare photo.

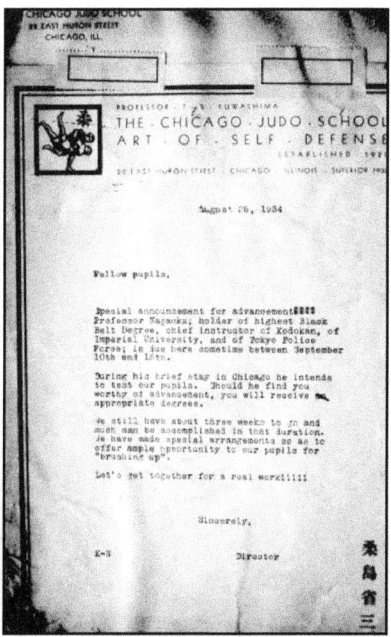

A letter to students at the Chicago judo school in 1934, informing them of Professor Nagaoka's visit, for the purpose of testing.

One of the earliest commercial judo schools in the United States was the Chicago Judo School, founded in 1920.
Here is one of their early advertising flyers from the early 1930s.

A photo of four early karate instructors in Hawaii in 1933, (l-r) Thomas Shigeru Miyashiro, Teru Azama, Kamesuke Higashionna and Seishin Ushara. Miyashiro was the first local sensei to make karate available to the public.

17

An Illustrated History Of Martial Arts In America – 1900 to Present

In 1935 Mel Bruno (standing 3rd from the left) became the fifth American to get a black belt in judo. He received this honor personally from Jigoro Kano. Above, Bruno is seen with a group of his earliest students.  *Courtesy of M. Bruno*

Master Jigoro Kano, founder of Kodokan Judo, visits the New York Judo Dojo in 1938. The dojo, which began in 1919, was run by George Yoshida for many years.

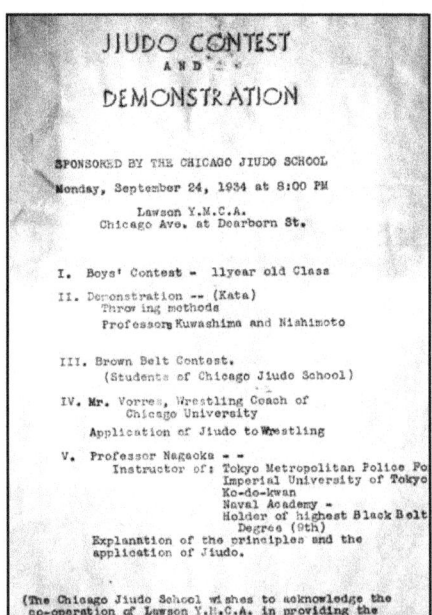

An early judo announcement, Chicago in 1934.

The 1930s

**NEW YORK DOJO (JUDO)**
AUTHORIZED BY KODO KWAN, TOKYO
FOUNDED 1921
135 WEST 51st STREET
NEW YORK CITY

ANNOUNCEMENT

September 18, 1935

The Executive Committee of the New York Dojo is honored and happy to announce that beginning this week, we are to have the full-time and regular services of Professor Kuwashima, 5th Degree Kodokan, as Head Instructor.

Prof. Kuwashima who has devoted his life to the study and furtherance of Judo, comes to us with a wealth of experience in teaching both Japanese and American peoples. Besides instructing in Mexico, being connected with Chicago University and training the Chicago police force, Prof. Kuwashima has conducted for the past fifteen years a Dojo in the latter city where more than 5,000 students have been enrolled in the study of Judo. During that time eighteen men who perservered received black belt degrees from the Kodokan and today maintain a Black Belt Degree Holders Association in Chicago.

Recently the Professor made a visit to Japan where honors were conferred by his college and the officials of the Kodokan in recognition of distinguished service rendered over the years and the high standards which he set in the furtherance of the art of Judo in America.

In welcoming Professor Kuwashima as Head Instructor, the Executive Committee wish to point out the almost unlimited possibilities in a city the size of New York for building this official branch of the Kodokan into one of the largest and most influential Dojos in the world. To that end we pledge to Professor Kuwashima our fullest co-operation and support.

Chairman of American Executive Committee

Chairman of the Japanese Executive Committee

Historical letter to its member from the New York Dojo.

Jigoro Kano at historic moment of 1936 Olympics in Berlin when American Jesse Owens was awarded a gold medal in the long jump after defeating Germany.

In 1937 a group of judo players and wrestlers from California are shown as they prepare to travel to Japan for training and competition.

Mel Bruno (3rd row, 5th from left) was the coach.

An Illustrated History Of Martial Arts In America – 1900 to Present

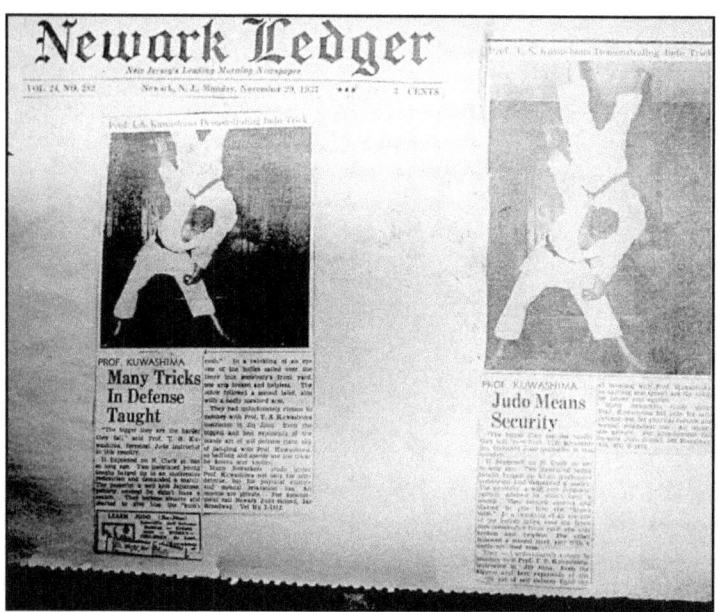

Early newspaper articles such as this from 1937 made the American public aware of judo, and by the mid 1930's most major American cities had at least one judo dojo. *Courtesy of Mel Bruno*

An article in this 1939 Sunday Mirror Magazine featured instructors from the New York Judo School demonstrating women's self defense.

In 1938 Mel Bruno (left) organized the first officially recognized college judo team in the U.S. It was at San Jose State.

The 1930s

In the 1930s many judo classes were held in high school gyms or rented auditoriums.

June Tegner, shown here training with judo expert Shozo Kuwashima in 1938, went on to be a major spokesperson for Judo for women. She was featured in dozens of major newspapers and mainstream magazines during the 1940s and 1950s extolling the benefits of judo for both self-defense and for a healthy lifestyle.

An Illustrated History Of Martial Arts In America – 1900 to Present

Danzan Ryu master Henry Okazaki (4th from left) with a number of his pupils in the mid-1930s in Hawaii.

Henry Okazaki (left) was one of the earliest ju-jutsu masters in Hawaii. He founded the Danzan-Ryu Ju-Jutsu system in the late 1930s and many of his students who moved to the United States mainland spread the system far and wide.

# The 1940s

With World War II going on, soldiers were again exposed to hand-to-hand combat, with plenty of ju-jutsu and judo techniques thrown in. By the end of the war, judo was widely known in the country and clubs were now numerous. Sport competition among judo clubs and organizations began after World War II and the number of judo players rose significantly

Between 1945 and 1950, a large number of ex-military personnel also began to open self-defense-oriented clubs. In cities like Boston, New York and Chicago, dozens of schools were teaching layman how to stop muggers with judo chops or intricate arm locks.

Karate was introduced to the mainland in 1946 by Robert Trias, but very few people practiced it. By the end of the '40s, almost every American knew what judo was and now a fair number of Caucasians had gained their black belts and were eagerly promoting the art.

# An Illustrated History Of Martial Arts In America – 1900 to Present

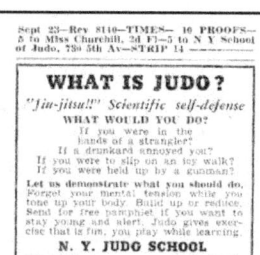

A 1940s advertisement from the New York Times promoting judo lessons.

A martial arts classic written at the height of World War II and peppered with anti-Japanese propaganda. Its premise is that with our American pioneer spirit we can beat the Japanese at their own game.

Judo pioneers Henry Stone (left) and Mel Bruno, were the first judo experts to promote collegiate judo competition in the United States. In 1940, Stone, who was coaching judo at U.C. Berkeley, and Bruno, the judo coach at San Jose State, held the first intercollegiate competition at San Jose State. Stone was also instrumental in forming the Beikoku Judo Yudanshakai – the first national judo organization in the United States. Stone also devised a weight system as early as 1948 and championed judo's inclusion into the Olympics, as well as having the AAU recognize Kodokan Judo as a sport. *Courtesy of Mel Bruno*

In the early 1940s military bases were teaching judo and ju-jutsu to most recruits. Here is a class being supervised by judo expert Mel Bruno, who is teaching a class at the Norfolk Naval training center in 1942.
*Courtesy of Mel Bruno.*

The 1940s

In 1942, the first comprehensive book on unarmed defense for military personnel was published by the United States government and covered all aspects of hand-to-hand combat.

Get Tough by British Major W.E Fairbairn, who was a former chief of police in Shanghai, first appeared in America in 1942. It was an excellent introduction to close-quarter combat, as taught to the U.S armed forces during World War II.

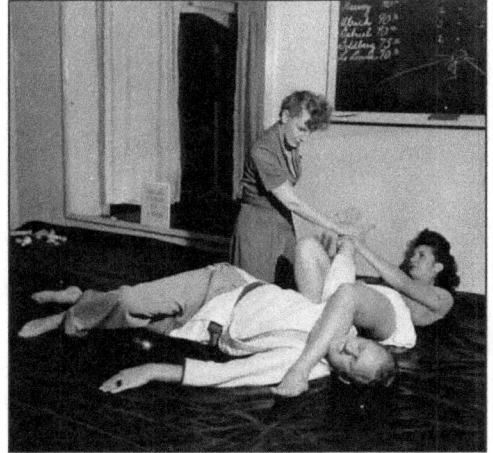

By the early 1940s there were a number of American female judo and ju-jutsu instructors teaching self-defense. Here, June Tegner teaches a private lesson in 1942

Charles Neal was the Jiu-Jitsu Advisor at NKJU. He began his training in 1940 under the likes of the late Professor Kiyose Nakae and John Styers. He also was instructed in the way of the kata by Master Hiroshige Yoshida.

Sensei Neal passed away on January 20, 1988

An Illustrated History Of Martial Arts In America – 1900 to Present

**Kill or Get Killed** was published in 1943.

Its author, Col. Rex Applegate, was one of America's leading authorities on close combat.

In the mid-1940s, he was in charge of close combat training at the Military Intelligence Training Center. Among his teachers were W.E. Fairbairn and E. A. Sykes of Shanghai Police and British Commando fame.

The book was widely used by the various military branches of the United States and Great Britain.

Mel Bruno (left) was instrumental in getting judo into American colleges and universities. Here he is teaching a group of Cornell University students in the early 1940s
*Courtesy of M. Bruno*

Charles Nelson was one of the earliest and best known self-defense instructors in New York city. An expert in hand-to-hand combat, which he learned in the Marine Corps, he opened his self defense academy in the late 1940s and taught thousands of students practical street effective combative techniques. He passed away in 2003 at age 88.

10th Degree Black Belt Ernie Cates, creator of Neko-Ryu Goshin Jitsu teaching a class. A retired Marine Captain, Cates began training in Judo and Ju-Jitsu in Okinawa in the 1940's and was Okinawa Judo Champion in 1956.

The 1940s

One of the earliest jiu-jitsu mass-market booklets was authored by I.C. King, an instructor in the United States Marines. It appeared in the early 1940s. Above, the cover and an inside page are shown.

One of the earlier books on self-defense, combining various martial arts of judo, ju jitsu, wrestling and boxing.

An article from the early 1940s in an American tabloid, showing the practical application of judo and ju-jutsu.

An Illustrated History Of Martial Arts In America – 1900 to Present

Hawaiian Kenpo pioneer William K.S. Chow (right) began teaching his art in 1944. A student of James Mitose, Chow became one of the top Hawaiian Senseis who trained a great number of black belts including Ed Parker, Adriano Emperado, Paul Yamaguchi and Ralph Castro. In this photo a young Ed Parker is seen on the left. *Courtesy of Ed Parker.*

Duke Moore (left) was one of the pioneers of martial arts in the U.S. He opened his famous American Judo and Ju-jitsu Academy in San Francisco in 1944. He was instrumental in the formation of the North-California Judo Association. In 1950 Moore trained with Mas Oyama and became one of the first American karate black belts. Over the years, he has elevated hundreds of black belts, who went on to teach all over the U.S.

Professor Duke Moore's (inset) famous dojo in San Francisco, which he opened in 1944. While here, he taught mostly judo and ju-jutsu at first, and produced some of the best black belts of the time.

Professor James Mitose (right) was one of the first and best-known Kenpo Karate instructors in Hawaii. In 1942, he organized the Official Self Defense Club in Honolulu, where he taught his Kosho-ryu Kenpo System until 1953, when Thomas Young (standing next to Mitose) took over. His most famous student was William K.S. Chow (in the dark gi).

The 1940s

The cover and an excerpt page from an early hand-to-hand combat manual published in 1945. Its price was 25 cents.

James Cagney (shown being thrown) with his judo teacher and co-star in **Blood on the Sun** Jack Sergil (aka John Harlan). Jack Sergil was a 3rd degree black belt before WWII as well as a police officer.

He trained during the 1940s and used his judo in the 1945 film, **Blood on the Sun**. In the movie, he defeats a Japanese police captain while trying to escape from Japan, after discovering the country's aim of world dominance.

The climactic fight scene depicts judo superbly.

An interesting photo in the Chicago Daily News promoting judo in 1946

In the late 1940s Prof. F.A. Matsuyama (above, inset) developed the Yawara stick, which became widely used by law enforcement personnel all over the country. In 1947, he published his first manual on the use of this weapon (above, left).

Adriano Emperado was one of the leading karate instructors in Hawaii during the late 1940s and 1950s.

An eclectic martial artist, Emperado began his training with escrima, then studied judo, kung fu and later became a student of William K.S. Chow.

He is one of the founding fathers of Kajukenbo, and has trained such well-known students as Al Dacascos, Al Gene Caraulia, Sid Asuncion, Tony Ramos and Ian Allred.

Al Holtmann was a pioneer of judo in Southern California. He taught in San Diego and was the first to teach aikido at his dojo in the U.S. He taught from 1946 until he passed away in 2001.

The 1940s

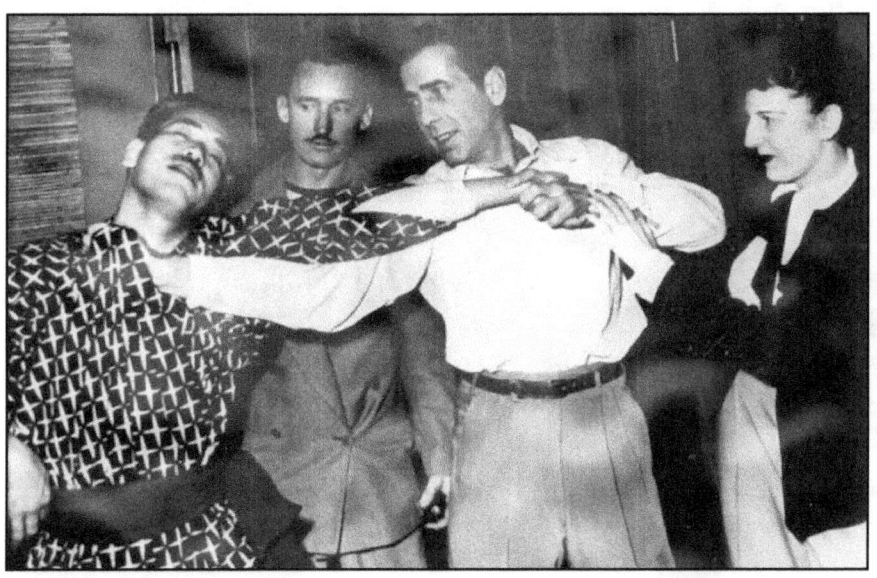

Members of the Tegner family, who ran a dojo in Hollywood, were the first legitimate black belts to choreograph fight scenes regularly in films. Jon, June, and Bruce worked with numerous stars beginning in the 1940s. Here, June Tegner is seen working with Humphrey Bogart. Husband, Jon, watches in the background.

Kiro Nagano one of the pioneers of judo in America came to the U.S in 1916 already an accomplished Judo champion. He captained the strong Southern California Judo team for 38 years, then became a top instructor and administrator

Newspaper photos and article such as these from the 1940s empowered many women to seek judo training around the country.

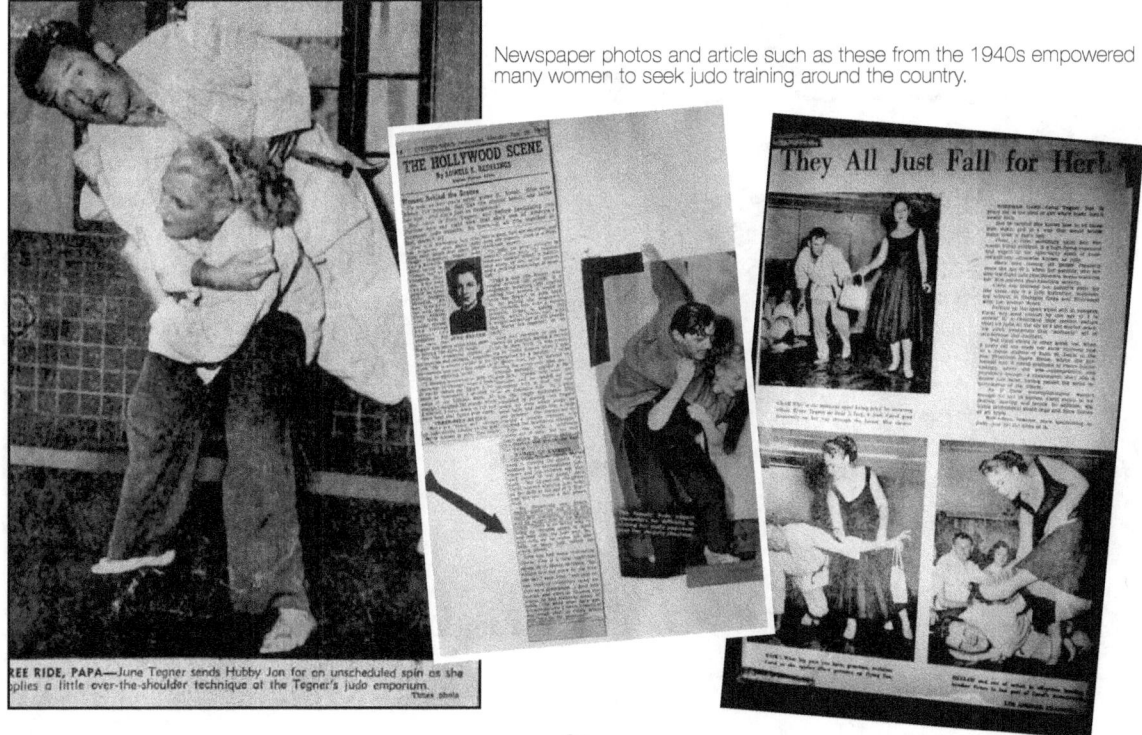

An Illustrated History Of Martial Arts In America – 1900 to Present

Father of American Karate, Robert Trias, shows the power of Karate in this demonstration during the late 1940s. Trias was the first American to teach karate here, when he opened a dojo in Phoenix, Arizona in 1946. In 1948, he founded the U.S. Karate Association which became the largest in the U.S. and was a leader of American karate until his death in 1983.

Paul Yamaguchi is one of the elder statesmen of Hawaiian martial arts. He studied under Henry Okazaki and was one of only six students to receive a black belt from James Mitose.

Duke Moore kneeling in front row (3rd from right) is seen in the late 1940s with some of his students.

Top right is a young Mel Augustine, who went on to be a leader in American judo.

Three early martial arts pioneers in Hawaii were (r-l): Joe Emperado, Adriano Emperado and Woodrow McCandless. In front is Mariano Tiwanaka, one of the early Black Belt students.

Original members of James Mitose's self defense club in Hawaii in 1948. Mitose is seen in dark robes in the back. Next to him (left) is William Chow. In the middle row, 2nd from right, is Arthur Keawa.

# The 1950s

This was the decade in which judo really took off and Americans were first exposed to the "deadly" art of karate.

Thanks largely to the Strategic Air Command whose leaders embraced judo as excellent training for airmen, many enlisted personnel began studying judo at Air Force bases around the country. Top-notch judo instructors from Japan came to the U.S and numerous Americans traveled to Japan for training. Major judo organizations began to spring up and judo became a recognized sport within the AAU.

It was during the early '50s that karate got its first real exposure in America, due to numerous karate experts from Japan who traveled here and demonstrated this deadly form of combat. Although by mid-1950s there were a few people teaching karate, it was still judo that Americans thought of when it came to self-defense.

Kung-fu, which was still practiced by Chinese mostly, was now beginning to be practiced by few non-Chinese students.

A large number of servicemen were stationed overseas, and many began studying the martial arts there.

Aikido was beginning to be practiced in Hawaii.

An Illustrated History Of Martial Arts In America – 1900 to Present

Comedian Bob Hope practices his Judo skills with Jon Tegner for preparation of the comedy thriller **My Favorite Spy**.   *Courtesy of Beverly Hills Archives*

Professor Sig Kufferath (1911-1999) was the headmaster of the Danzan-Ryu Ju-jutsu system. He began training under Henry S. Okazaki in Hawaii in 1937 and became Okazaki's most senior student. He took over leadership of the system after Okazaki's death in 1951.

Mel Augustine, shown demonstrating self-defense applications of judo at Fairchild Air Force Base (circa 1950) was one of the first judo instructors in the Strategic Air Command. He later became a well-known competitor and then president of the Northern California Judo Association. He was also vice-president of the U.S. Judo Federation.

The 1950s

## JUDO... UNEQUALLED AS A SELF DEFENSE
### ★ A SUPERB SPORT ★
### NEW JUDO CLASSES NOW STARTING
BRING THIS CARD AND RECEIVE YOUR
### FIRST LESSON FREE

STREET DEFENSE COURSE    REFRESHER COURSE

PRIVATE LESSONS FOR FAST AND COMPLETE LEARNING

### CALL NOW: HO. 2-9222
BE OUR GUEST AT HOLLYWOOD BRANCH
### NATIONAL JUDO SCHOOLS
5544 SUNSET BLVD. (Near Western Ave.)    HOLLYWOOD, CALIF.

This was a promotional postcard sent out by Bruce Tegner in 1951, promoting judo. Tegner's school in Hollywood was the most successful dojo of its time, with hundreds of members – some of which were well known Hollywood celebrities. *Courtesy of Beverly Hills Archives*

John Osako was one of the leading judo instructors and champions in the U.S. He was twice Pan American judo champion (1952, 1956), three-time AAU National champion (1955, 56, 58) and was the coach of the 1965 American team to the world championships. He was a certified international Judo Federation referee and served on various American judo committees. He was the chief instructor at the Detroit judo club, one of the largest in the U.S.

Judo and hand-to-hand combat expert Mel Bruno (left) was one of the only Americans to actually receive instruction from Gichin Funakoshi (right), father of modern karate. A pioneer of Judo in America, Bruno was one of the highest ranked non-Japanese judoka, who became supervisor of Judo and Combative Measures for the Strategic Air Command (SAC) in 1951. He was instrumental in bringing some of Japan's leading martial artists to the United States a few years later. The group toured Air Force bases throughout the country and were responsible for the growth of judo in the military. Bruno was the coach of the U.S. judo teams in the World Judo Championships in 1958 and 1961.

Kenzo Uyeno was a leading judo instructor and administrator who was instrumental in organizing the Capital Judo Black Belt Federation (Shufu Yudanshahai) in 1954. He was also president of the Judo Black Belt Federation of America (1962–63).

An Illustrated History Of Martial Arts In America – 1900 to Present

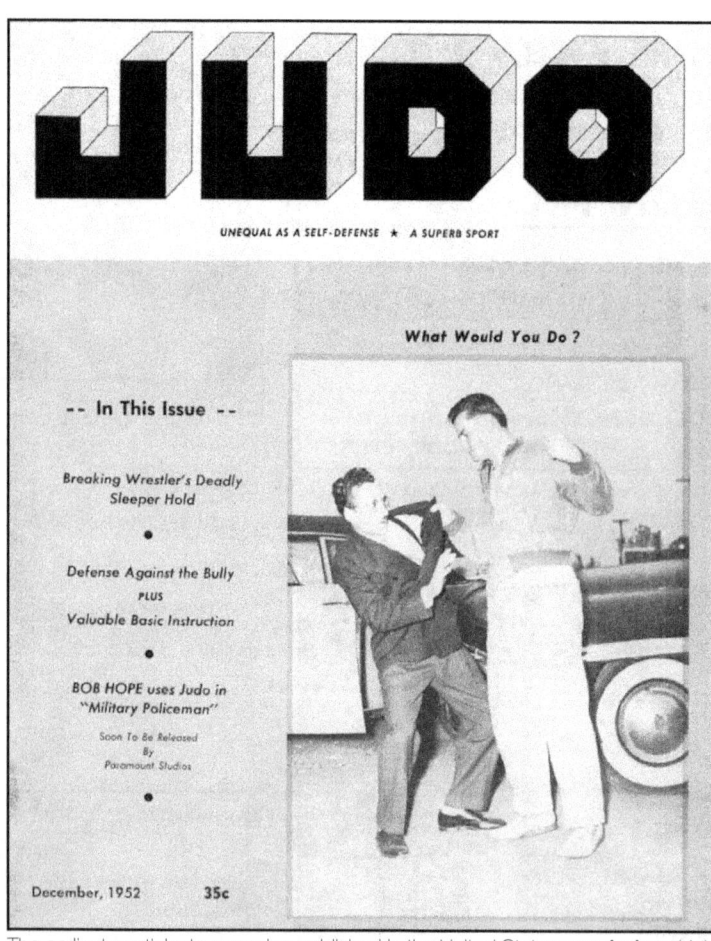

The earliest martial arts magazine published in the United States was **Judo**, which came out in 1952 and was founded by the Tegner family.

This book by James Mitose, first published in 1953, was the first book in English on Kempo karate. It was the first book to demonstrate karate techniques to the general public.

A 1953 newspaper article about U.S. Airmen studying the martial arts.

American-born Yosh Uchida was one of the major judo coaches and administrators in the U.S. He began teaching at San Jose State in 1937, and over the years, the university won 40 out of 44 national collegiate team titles. Uchida was mainly responsible for getting the AAU to accept judo as a sport in 1953. In 1962, he organized the first national collegiate championships and in 1964 became the first U.S. Olympic Judo coach.

The 1950s

In 1953 some of Japan's leading martial artists visited March Air Force Base where they demonstrated their fighting skills to hundreds of Airmen. In the front line (center with glasses) is Professor Sumiyuki Kotani, one of Japan's foremost judo masters. *Courtesy of Mel Bruno.*

1958 - Field House Marine Corps Base (Camp LeJeune, North Carolina): All Marine Judo Team coached and taught by The Legendary Ernie Cates (back row, first from right). Top row left to right: Howard George, Eugene Rodrequez, Little Joe Fournier', Melvin Meyers, Unidentified General 1 and 2, Karate Legend Don Nagle, Jim Lyles , ?, and Grandmaster Ernie Cates. Kneeling left to right: Bud McKain, ?, Bob Greene, Professor Ronald Duncan, G/Sgt Harris, Corporal Spellman, Frenchie Rodechaud, ?,G/Sgt Burke.

An Illustrated History Of Martial Arts In America – 1900 to Present

In 1953, at the invitation of the U.S. Air Force, some of Japan's top martial arts masters visited the U.S. giving demonstrations and holding seminars. Here, the group is at a stopover at Yosemite Park. Some of the famous masters include: (l-r standing) third from left H. Nishiyama (karate), 4th T. Ishikawa (judo), 6th I. Obata (karate), 7th K. Hosokawa (taihojutsu), 9th S. Kotani (Head of Foreign Section at Kodokan),10th K. Kobayashi (judo), 12th K. Tomiki (aikido)
Kneeling (l-r): 1st T. Kamada (karate), 6th T. Otaki (karate)
At top left is Emilio Bruno, head of S.A.C. Combative Measures and the man responsible for the tour.

Photo taken at the first National A.A.U. Judo Championships in 1953. Standing (l-r): J. Knight, A. Holtman, D. Carolla, S. Luke, R. Smith, C. Jerkow, K. Misuho, D. Draeger, K. Kuniyuki. Seated: D. Suketaro, H. Stone, and U. Yoshihiro.  *Courtesy Mel Bruno.*

The 1950s

This was an ad put out by the Strategic Air Command in 1953 promoting the demonstration by some of Japan's greatest martial arts masters. These types of demos were held in numerous air force bases around the country and helped spur the growth of martial arts in the U.S.

*Courtesy of M. Bruno.*

Mas Oyama was the first Oriental karate master to visit the U.S. and demonstrate his incredible skills. From March to November 1952, Oyama toured the whole country where he challenged and defeated professional wrestlers and boxers while also demonstrating the incredible breaking power of karate. This was the first major exposure the American public got to karate.

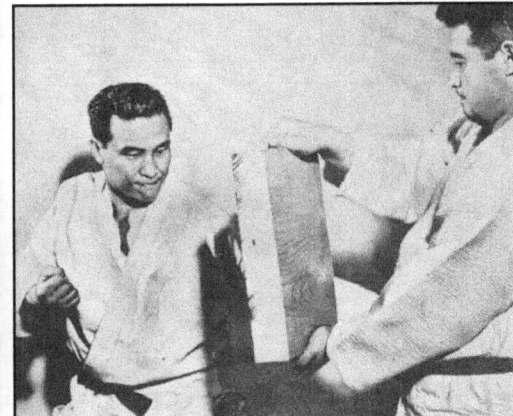

The Robert Trias dojo in Phoenix, Arizona, was opened in 1946 and was the first karate school in the continental U.S. In front is Robert Trias with his daughter Roberta. *Courtesy of P. Robino*

An Illustrated History Of Martial Arts In America – 1900 to Present

The first group of American Airmen practice karate in Tokyo in 1953, while some of Japan's top karate instructor's watch.

On the left is Obata Sensei and third from left is Nakayama Sensei.

Working out is Sgt. Daniel Matthies (left) and Sgt. Edwin Maley.

Twenty-two SAC members took the course.

*Courtesy of Mel Bruno.*

The first martial arts themed comic book "**Judo Joe**" was released in 1953.

By the early 1950s, judo became increasingly popular with law enforcement agencies because of its emphasis on close quarter combat.

The 1950s

Three early martial arts pioneers on the East Coast include Michael Depasquale (left), Junji Saito (center) and Pete Serengano.

The first studio owned by Ed Parker opened in Pasadena in 1956. Parker raised and renovated the original building, making it into a custom karate school.   *Courtesy of James Holzer.*

Koichi Tohei (center), one of Japan's foremost aikido experts, helped popularize Aikido in Hawaii in the early 1950s, when he visited the Islands and held numerous demonstrations and seminars.

Before the Korean War most hand to hand combat training in the U.S. Military was based on Jiu-jitsu techniques.

41

# An Illustrated History Of Martial Arts In America – 1900 to Present

This was the first judo tournament ever conducted by a U.S. military organization. The winners went on to represent SAC at the 1954 AAU Nationals.

Welcoming speeches by the heads of SAC at the first Strategic Air Command Judo Tournament.

Coach Walter Todd accepts the Kodokan Banner from General Curtis E. LeMay, after his airmen won SAC's first judo tournament in 1954. From left to right: Professor Otaki, General LeMay, W. Todd, M. Curtis (overall champion) and Professor Kotani.

American judo champion Vince Tamura was a national judo champion in 1954, '56 and '59. He competed in the 1956 World Championships and opened a dojo in Dallas in 1960 where thousands of students have studied under him. He is a noted self-defense specialist.
*Courtesy of Fred Degerburg*

The 1950s

By the early 1950s, American children were practicing Judo – not for competition, but for fun or self-defense.

Above, in the 1955 film **Bad Day at Black Rock**, Spencer Tracy plays a one-armed stranger, who comes to a tiny town possessing a terrible past, they want to keep secret. In the movie, Tracy uses his jiu-jutsu skills to defeat one of the violent towns folk.

The first martial arts demonstration on a live T.V. show was on the Arthur Godfrey Show in the early 1950s. Mel Bruno, one of America's top judo black belts, demonstrated the art to millions of Americans. Godfrey is sitting on the right.
*Courtesy of Mel Bruno*

Florendo Visitacion (left) was one of the earliest leading ju-jutsu instructors on the East Coast. In 1955, he founded the Vee Jitsu style of ju-jutsu and continued to teach in the New York area for over 30 years. He is seen here with one of his famous students, Moses Powell.
*Courtesy of Official Karate.*

An Illustrated History Of Martial Arts In America – 1900 to Present

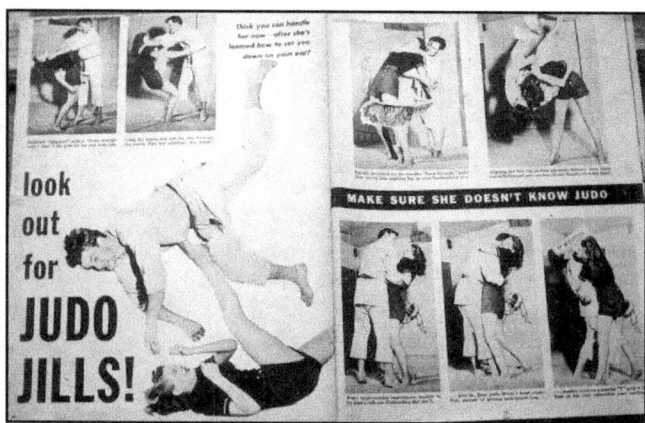

In the early 1950s Life Magazine featured this article on judo for women.

In the early 1950s, ju-jitsu classes were starting to get popular, especially in the big cities where crime was constantly increasing.

Bruce Tegner, seen here throwing one of his students, was a California State Judo Champion in the early 1950s and founded his own Jukado martial arts system. He specialized in teaching self-defense and was one of the first instructors in the United States to teach blind and disabled people. He is probably best known for the numerous books he authored on the various martial arts, including karate, kung fu, savate and aikido.

During the early 1950s, a group of airmen take classes at one of the United States air bases. On the left watching is Simiyuki Kotani, one of Japan's leading instructors.

The 1950s

In early 1950s some of Japan's top judo instructors came to the United States and demonstrated their skills at various Air Force bases across the country. Here a group of airmen watch one of the demos.   *Courtesy of Mel Bruno*

Hawaiian-born Gordon Doversola was one of the first karate instructors on the West Coast. An Okinawa-te stylist, he opened a dojo in Los Angeles in 1957, and taught such well known students as Joe Lewis, Bob Wall and Jim Kelly.

Doversola was one of the earliest martial artists to choreograph fight scenes for movies. In 1962 he trained Frank Sinatra for a martial arts fight scene in the **Manchurian Candidate**.

American Karate pioneer William J. Dometrich, who studied Chito-ryu karate under the style's founder Dr. Tsuyoshi Chitose, was one of the first Americans to teach karate in the U.S.

In 1955 he began teaching at Fairmont State College, West Virginia and in 1967 he formed an American National Chito-ryu Organization.

A convert to Zen Buddhism, Dometrich worked in law enforcement and has continued to teach and promote karate tirelessly. He is one of the most respected senseis of traditional karate in the United States.

Rick Lenchus was one of the first martial arts instructors in New York City.   *Courtesy of Official Karate*

Pete Siringano *(seen here on the cover of Masters of Self Defense)* was one of the first ju-jitsu and combat karate instructors in New York City. He opened the Staten Island Ju-Jitsu and Karate dojo in 1956. He taught Goshindo Kempo karate and Samurai Ju-Jitsu till he passed away in 1994 at age 66. The City of New York honored him by naming the intersection outside his former dojo Grandmaster Peter Siringano Sr. Square.

Cecil Patterson was the pioneer of Wado-ryu karate in the United States. He learned the art in Japan while stationed there with the Navy. Upon his return to the United States, he opened the first karate dojo in the state of Tennessee in 1957, in his hometown of Seveierville. In 1968, he founded the United States Eastern Wado-Kai Federation. He passed away in 2002.

Dr. Sachio Ashida was a top judo competitor in Japan before emigrating to the U.S. in 1953, where he became a leading instructor and administrator. In 1960 he founded the Midwest Judo Yudanshahai and has been involved in every aspect of judo since then. In 1976 Dr. Ashida was selected as the lead coach for the U.S. Olympic team.

The 1950s

Tsutomu Oshima, seen here delivering a flying side kick, was the first Japanese instructor to teach Shotokan Karate in the United States. Oshima settled in Los Angeles in 1955 and, a year later, opened his first dojo. He established Shotokan Karate of America, the first Shotokan organization in the United States. In 1958 he began his annual Nisei Week Karate Championships, which is still in existence.

In 1957, two of Japan's top Judo senseis, Professor Kotani (3rd from the left) and Professor Hosokawa (5th from the left) were invited to Barksdale Air Force Base to help with training and to conduct SAC Airforce-wide Judo Tournaments. Between the two senseis is Mel Bruno and to the extreme right is Pop More. *Courtesy of M. Bruno*

Frank Goody Jr. was the first to teach karate in Colorado. He opened a dojo in Boulder as early as 1957 and has taught most of the karate pioneers of the area.

Hawaiian karate pioneer Bobby Lowe, opened the first Kyokushin Kai dojo outside of Japan in 1957. Before becoming a student of Mas Oyama in 1952, Lowe had trained with Henry Okazaki, and became one of only a few students to get a black belt from James Mitose.

Walter Todd was one of the earliest martial arts instructors in the U.S. He trained judo in Japan in the late '40s with Kyuzo Mifune and later became the first foreigner to train with Ohtsuka sensei (the founder of Wado-Ryu karate). In 1948 he opened a dojo in Northern California and, in 1951, Mel Bruno hired him to teach judo at the air force. Besides judo and karate, Todd also became a high ranking aikido expert. He passed away in 1999. He's seen here teaching judo to George Harris.
*Courtesy of Mel Bruno*

Kiyoshi Nakae was considered the dean of American Jiu jitsu. A teacher for over 50years his best selling book **Jiu Jitsu Complete** was a classic. He taught thousands of Americans first in Chicago, then in Greenwich Village. He passed away in 1963 at age 79.

As early as the mid 1950's most police academies were training all their recruits in Judo and Ju Jitsu techniques.

## The 1950s

Ron Duncan was one of the early pioneers of martial arts on the East Coast. He began teaching in New York in the mid-1950s and was noted for his skills with numerous weapons. Many claim he was the first to introduce ninjutsu to the United States.
*Courtesy of Carlos Velez II*

Don Angier (left) was one of the earliest instructors of the Samurai arts in the United States. Headquartered on the West Coast, Angier who began teaching in the 1950s, is the inheritor of Yanagi Ryu Aiki Jujitsu of the Yoshida family. The system Yanagi ryu Aiki Bugei is a complete Samurai art encompassing all the skills that the Samurai had to know to execute their duties. Angier is one of the Western World's most knowledgeable aiki jutsu instructors.

Ari Anestadias was the first person to teach karate in Canada. The former JKA student began to teach in Montreal in the mid 1950s.

# An Illustrated History Of Martial Arts In America – 1900 to Present

A photo of a typical karate dojo in the late 1950's and early 1960's. Often due to cheap rent, these dojos were large windowless rooms with hardwood floors and little equipment.

Mel Bruno (right) presents a plaque to General S. Power, commander in chief of the Strategic Air Command from the Kodokan for the General's outstanding contribution to the sport of judo in America. Power was a 3rd degree black belt in judo. *Courtesy of M. Bruno.*

Philip Porter (2nd from the left in the front row) was one of the leaders of American Judo in the 1950s and '60s. He helped found the United States Judo Association in 1954 and was the National Chairman of the AAU Judo Committee from 1961-1964. He was also the chairman of the United States Olympic Judo Committee from 1964 to 1968. In 1995, he founded his own organization, The United States Martial Arts Association. In the photo are some of America's top Judo men of the 1960s: (front row, l-r): Charles Lambur, P. Porter, K.Kuniyuki, Shinahara. Back Row: G.Harris, H. Nishioka, T. Seino.

One of the earliest Hollywood celebrities to get a black belt in karate was Ricky Nelson (left) who studied with Bruce Tegner (right) in the late 1950s. In March of 1961, Nelson displayed his karate to millions of Americans on the popular T.V. show **The Adventures of Ozzie and Harriet**. *Courtesy of Beverly Hills Archives*

# The 1950s

Peter Urban was one of the pioneers of karate in the United States. A student of Gogen "the Cat" Yamaguchi, Urban opened a dojo on the East Coast in the late 1950s and became one of the best-known instructors in America. In the 1960s he founded his own U.S.A. Goju system, which for years was among the biggest karate associations in the New York area. In 1961, Urban promoted the first karate tournament on the East Coast, "The Peter Urban Open Karate Tournament" held at New York's Manhattan Center. Over the years, Urban has taught some of the leading martial artists on the East Coast, among them: Chuck Merriman, Aaron Banks, Al Gotay, William Lui, Frank Ruiz, Ron Van Clief, Joe Hess and John Kuhl.

*Courtesy of Beverly Hills Archives*

Jimmy H. Woo (sitting second from left) is the founder of the kung fu San Soo system. He moved to the U.S from China in 1935, and was one of the first men to teach Kung fu publicly on a large scale. He was headquartered in South California until his death in 1992.

Four top Air Force judo champions in the late 1950s. Back center: Williams, (left) Boone, (right) R. Reeves, (kneeling) T. Seiro. *Courtesy of Mel Bruno.*

# An Illustrated History Of Martial Arts In America – 1900 to Present

Takaniko Ishikawa, seen here as he is about to throw his opponent, was twice All-Japan Judo Champion (1949-50) who came to the United States in 1957 at the invitation of the United States Air Force. He settled on the East Coast and became one of the leading judo instructors in the country. He influenced a large number of America's top judo competitors.

Below, James Miyagi is the elder states man of Shorinji-ryu karate in Hawaii. He opened his Ken Shukan dojo in 1957 and has been affiliated with Richard Kim ever since.

Written by Robert Trias. An early American pioneer.

Jhoon Rhee, the father of Taekwondo in America, began teaching in Texas in 1958. He moved to Washington D.C. in 1962 establishing a chain of very successful dojos. He is the inventor of the foam rubber safe-T-equipment, and is noted for the numerous champions he has taught, among them: Allen Steen, Jeff Smith, Pat Burleson, Gordon Franks, Larry Carnahan, Pat Worley and John Chung. He is undoubtedly the best known and respected taekwondo Master in the U.S.

Mas Tsuroka, known as the father of Canadian Karate, opened his first dojo in Toronto in 1958. A black belt in Chito Ryu Karate, Tsuroka sponsored the Canadian Karate Championships in 1962, one of the first major tournaments in North America. His numerous black belts helped spread the art all over Canada.

The 1950s

George Mattson introduced Uechi-ryu karate to the United States in 1958. One of the best-known and respected early karate instructors, Mattson wrote **The Way of Karate** in 1963, one of the first karate books by an American sensei. In 1990, Mattson founded the International Uechi-ryu Federation and became its president. He is headquartered in the Boston area.

Published in 1959, this was the first mass-market paperback book on karate. Many leading senseis across the U.S. admit that it was this book, by Bruce Tegner, that brought their first students into their dojos.

A former high school science teacher and judo instructor, Sam Allred started the first public school judo club in the United States in 1959. A resident of Albuquerque, New Mexico, Allred began studying kajukenbo in the early 1960s and became the first non-Hawaiian to earn a black belt in this art. In the 1970s Allred promoted a number of top ten karate tournaments and was one of the leading instructors in the southwest for many years.

This photo taken, in 1958, is the first group of students graded by Shotokan master Tsutomu Oshima (seated in front). Two seats to his left is George Takahashi and sixth from the left is famous judo expert, Hayward Nishioka, who later received a black belt in karate from Oshima. A young Caylor Adkins, who became karate chairman for the AAU (1974-77) is seated in the back row third from the right, and Jordan Roth is second from left.   *Courtesy of Caylor Adkins*

An Illustrated History Of Martial Arts In America – 1900 to Present

Isshin-ryu karate was introduced to the United States by Don Nagle in the late 1950s. A student of Tatsuo Shimabuku (right), Nagle was one of the first Americans on the East Coast to teach karate and was one of the pioneers in the art. Many of the East Coast's leading senseis and champions were among his students. *Courtesy of Gary Alexander*

The golden age of judo in America was between 1955 and 1965 when thousands of Americans, many in the armed forces, were practicing and competing.

The 1950s

George Harris (right) was one of America's top judo competitors in the 1950s and 1960s. He was United States heavyweight champion in 1957, 1958, 1960 and 1961. He was also overall champion in 1957, 1958 and 1961. A former member of the Strategic Air Command where he began his training, Harris has been one of the leaders of the Armed Force's judo program. *Courtesy of M. Bruno*

American karate pioneer, Dan Ivan, was one of the first servicemen to study the martial arts right after the war, while stationed in Japan. A member of the Army's Criminal Investigation Division, Ivan stayed in Japan from 1948-1956 and was one of the first Americans to open a dojo in Southern California during the late 1950s. It was Ivan who brought famous karate master Fumio Demura to the United States in 1965, and the two partnered in establishing a large number of dojos. *Courtesy of Official Karate*

Karate classes in the late 1950s were often given at judo dojos. Here, a karate class is taught by Ed Hamile, one of the earliest karate instructors on the Hawaiian Islands.

# The 1960s

    This was the decade of karate and, in these 10 years, Americans embraced this new martial art by the thousands. Numerous American servicemen who studied karate while stationed in the Orient returned and began teaching it.
    Although judo for most of the decade was still a highly visible martial art, it was karate that the masses were intrigued with. The board and brick breaking, the kicking and the almost superhuman power of black belt karate men hooked Americans. Television viewers were exposed to karate on numerous shows and books were published by the dozens on the subject.
    Other arts were also getting exposure, especially kung-fu, due mostly to Bruce Lee's **"Green Hornet"** TV series. Thanks to martial arts magazines like **Black Belt**, which began in 1961, arts such as aikido, kendo, iaido got write-ups, but these arts were just in the background. Karate ruled the decade. Tournaments flourished and major American karate champions became highly visible. A large number of top Oriental instructors emigrated to the U.S. and helped to propagate the art.

## The 1960s

Bruce Tegner, right, was one of the earliest pioneers of karate in the U.S. A martial arts student from an early age, (both his parents were judo black belts), Tegner became famous when he wrote the first mass paperback book on karate in 1960, which, according to many karate pioneers, made students seek them out and undoubtedly helped the growth of karate in America.

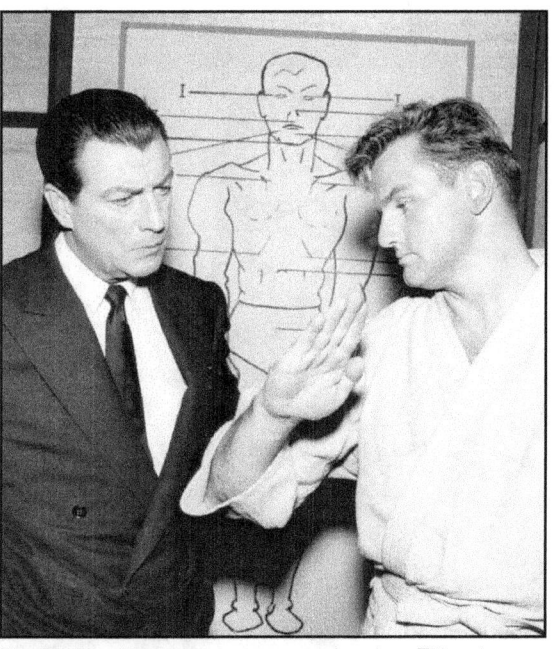

The first time Karate was seen on an American T.V. series was on January 8,1960, on **The Detectives** starring Robert Taylor (seen here on the left). In one of the episodes entitled 'Karate', Detective Matt Holbrook (Taylor) must track down a killer who is killing his victims with deadly blows to the neck. In the episode, Bruce Tegner (right) plays a karate expert who explains the potential power of karate and even demonstrates how a 'karate chop' can break a brick.

One of the first mass market booklets on judo was published in the early 1960s by the Athletic Institute, a non-profit organization devoted to the advancement of athletics and recreation. The Institute published over 30 titles on various sports. The consultant to the book was Sadoki Nakabayashi, 7th Dan.

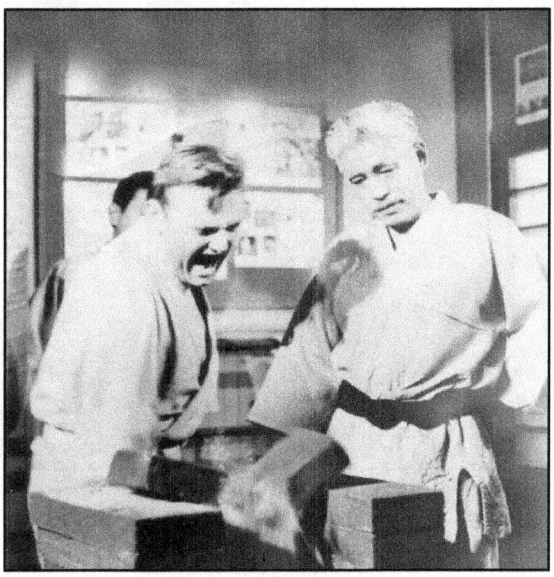

# An Illustrated History Of Martial Arts In America – 1900 to Present

This book, written by Hidetaka Nishiyama, was the first book published in the U.S. that demonstrated the art of karate with clear, easy-to-follow photos, written by a true master. Published in 1960, the book became an instant best-seller and made Nishiyama famous world-wide, helping to make him one of the earliest leaders of karate in the U.S.

Tony Ramos, a Hawaiian Kajukenbo instructor, was one of the first karate instructors in Southern California, moving to Los Angeles in 1960.

American karate champion Gary Alexander accepts congratulations from Kyokushinkai grandmaster Mas Oyama, after winning the 1st North American Karate Championships in 1962, in New York City.

In 1960, Phillip Koeppel founded the first karate club in the state of Illinois, the Peoria Judo and Karate Center. Koeppel began his training in Japan, while in the navy and upon his return to the United States, opened his dojo. He joined the U.S.K.A. under Robert Trias. In 1984 he founded his own organization called, "The United States Karate Do Kai." In the photo, Koeppel (center in the back) is seen with his earliest group of students.

The 1960s

Elvis Presley was undoubtedly the most famous entertainer to study the martial arts. He got his black belt in karate in 1960 from Hank Slemansky, then continued his training with numerous instructors, including Ed Parker, shown here.

During the 1950s and '60s, commercial judo clubs like Hal Sharp's dojo in Los Angeles, was common in most big cities. Today, few clubs like this exist.

Maynard Miner was the first Shotokan karate instructor in New York City. He trained in Tokyo with the Japan Karate Association in the mid 1950s and opened his first dojo in Brooklyn in 1960. Famous New York sensei George Cofield was Miner's student.

**The Case of the Dangerous Robin** was the first American T.V. series to feature karate on a regular basis. The show which aired in 1961, starred Rick Jason playing a freelance insurance investigator Robin Scott who was a karate expert. Jason (right) studied karate with Ed Parker for many years and used sensei Parker as the shows fight choreographer.

Shotokan Karate pioneer, Randall Hassell, was the first instructor to open a Shotokan dojo in the St. Louis area in 1962. In 1984, he broke away from the JKA and formed the American JKA Association and, four years later founded the American Shotokan Karate Alliance.

The first large traditional karate tournament in the United States took place in 1961 at the Los Angeles Sports Arena. The event, which was called The All America Tournament of Karate was produced by Hidetaka Nishiyama. James Yabe won the event.. *Courtesy of A.A.K.F.*

The 1960s

The first issue of **Black Belt Magazine** appeared in December of 1961 and measured a scant 5 by 8 inches (**Reader's Digest** size). It contained 64 pages of news and articles on the various martial arts. The magazine was founded by James and Mito Uyehara and Lou Kimcey. Eventually Mito took over as publisher, and, by 1965, the magazine became a monthly publication.

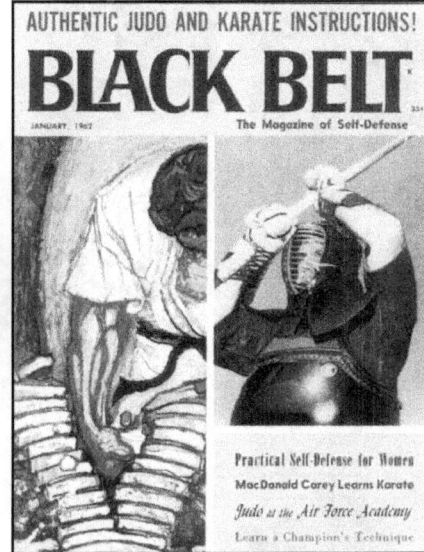

The second issue of **Black Belt Magazine** went to full size (8.5" x 11") and contained 65 pages and cost 35 cents.

World famous karate master Mas Oyama presented a spectacular breaking demo that awed the audience at the North American Karate Tournament held at Madison Square Gardens on November 24, 1962. American Isshin-ryu instructor, Gary Alexander won the event. This was one of the first large karate tournaments held in the United States. *Courtesy of Gary Alexander*

Some of the East Coast's top karate experts pose with Mas Oyama at the North American Karate Tournament held at Madison Square Gardens on November 24, 1962. Oyama's Kyokushinkai organization sponsored the event. Top (l-r): E. Alexander, Don Nagle, Mas Oyama, and Peter Urban. Kneeling: Jerry Bucholz, Gary Alexander (winner of the event) and E. Doyle.    *Courtesy of Gary Alexander*

An Illustrated History Of Martial Arts In America – 1900 to Present

Washin-ryu karate instructor, Hidy Ochai, who came to the United States in 1962, became one of the most visible instructors due to his spectacular demonstrations at tournaments all over the United States. He also established one of the largest and most successful dojos on the East Coast.

World-famous Shotokan karate instructor Hidetaka Nishiyama came to the United States in 1961 and became one of the earliest leaders of American karate. Settling in Los Angeles, he soon established the All-American Karate Federation, which became one of the largest karate groups in the United States. In 1968, he established the International Amateur Karate Federation, which has become one of the largest Traditional Karate Organizations in the world. In 1960, Nishiyama authored **Karate: The Art of Empty Hand Fighting**, one of the first books on the subject and still considered by many to be the definitive text.

Teruyuki Okazaki was one of the leading Shotokan karate instructors in Japan, when he moved to the United States in 1961. A representative of the Japan Karate Association, he settled in Philadelphia and pioneered Shotokan karate on the East Coast. In the early 1960s, he organized the East Coast Collegiate Karate Union and, in 1977, he founded the International Shotokan Karate Federation, which has branches in over 30 countries.

The 1960s

Twice All-Japan Karate Champion in Kumite, Takayuki Mikami came to the United States as a representative of the Japan Karate Association in 1963. One of the world's foremost experts in Shotokan Karate, Mikami moved to New Orleans where he has taught thousands of students without compromising his original roots. Known as a top referee, Mikami oversees a large organization and is widely respected by many American Karate instructors because of his open-minded attitude.

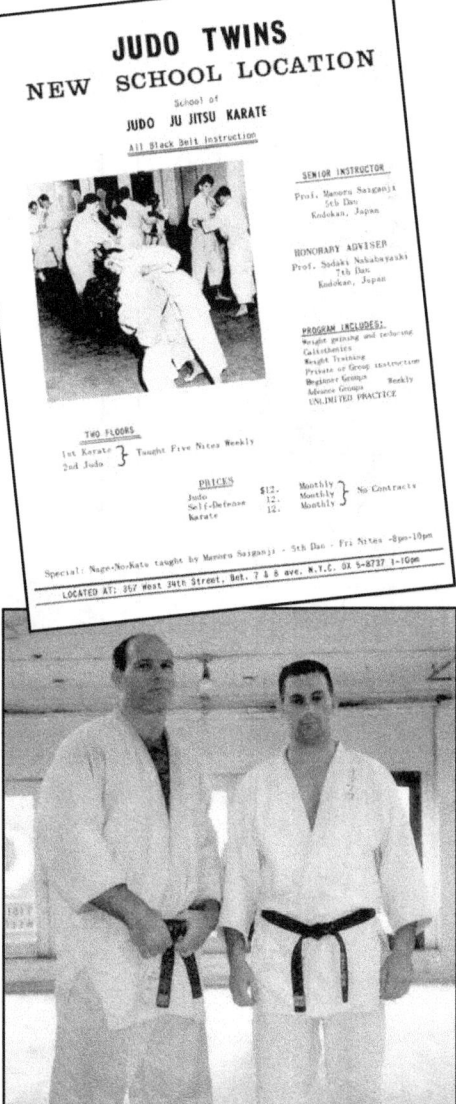

Haeng Ung Lee was a Korean American taekwondo pioneer founder of the American Taekwondo Association (A.T.A.). In 1962 he moved to the United States, brought here by a former student, Richard Reed. The two founded the ATA in 1966 and it eventually grew into one of the largest martial arts organizations in the United States with over 250,000 students.

Bernie Lepkofker (left), seen here with a young Chuck Merriman, ran one of the best-known judo dojos – The Judo Twins – in New York City during the early 1960s. The Judo Twins were two of the first dojos that began to offer karate classes in the New York area. Peter Urban, one of the founders of karate on the East Coast, began to teach at Lepkofker's school before opening his own dojo.

Brandon Lai was one of the early pioneers of kung fu in America. He came to the United States in 1961 as an expert in the Northern Praying Mantis System and opened a martial arts supply company. He was instrumental in promoting kung fu in its infancy, especially on the West Coast of the United States, and was an executive advisory council member of the AAU National Kung Fu Committee.

David Moon was a Texas-based karate champion during the 1960s. He was a 3-time United States Karate Champion who was invited by the Mexican government to help develop their sports and physical activity programs. Moon now runs one of the most successful organizations in that country.

One of the world's most renowned and respected Shotokan Karate masters, Hirokazu Kanazawa, who won the All-Japan Karate Championships three times in a row, he was one of the first Japanese to teach his art in America. He taught classes in Honolulu, Hawaii from 1960 to 1963.

Robert Fusaro was one of the first Americans to teach Shotokan karate in the U.S. He studied in Japan during the 1950s with the JKA and, in 1960, opened his first dojo in Minneapolis. He is affiliated with H. Nishiyama and is, today, one of the most respected and highest ranked instructors in the U.S. *Courtesy of Robert Fusaro*

Texas karate champion Roy Kurban (shown delivering a side kick to Cecil Peoples) is one of the leading American tournament fighters. Between 1966 and 1977 he won one hundred and seventeen awards in national and international competition. A student of Allen Steen and Skipper Mullins, Kurban was one of the most liked competitors on the American Karate Circuit before he retired to Arlington, Texas, where he runs his American Black Belt Academy.

The 1960s

Professor Wally Jay, shown demonstrating an arm bar, was one of the most influential martial artists in the United States since his induction into the Black Belt Hall of Fame in 1969. A student of famous Hawaiian ju jitsu master Henry Okazaki, Professor Jay founded his own Small Circle Ju Jitsu System in 1987, which has been widely practiced world-wide. Over the years he has taught thousands of students, among them Bruce Lee.

Ray Dalke was one of the top Shotokan karate competitors of the mid- and late-1960s. A protégé of Hidetaka Nishiyama, Dalke was one of the few students to graduate the grueling JKA instructor's course. For many years, he ran the martial arts program at the University of Riverside, which became one of the largest in the country. Besides sparring, Dalke was also a superb kata competitor. He is seen here at one of the early traditional tournaments.

Louis Delgado (left) was one of the leading karate champions in the U.S. during the late 1960s and early 1970s. He was noted for his aggressive offensive fighting style as well as his beautiful kata performances. An East Coaster, Delgado studied with many of East Coast's leading karate instructors, among them Frank Ruiz and Peter Urban. At this East Coast tournament world Champion Joe Lewis (in the gi standing on the left) and Chuck Norris (in the gi sitting behind the referee) watch the competition.

Burmese American martial arts instructor Maung Gyi (center) came to the United States in 1960 and introduced Bando to America. In 1968, he founded the American Bando Association. He is seen here at a tournament in 1970 being flanked by Kim Soo Jin (left) and Robert Trias. Gyi has authored numerous books on Bando and Kickboxing.

On March 29, 1961, Ricky Nelson demonstrated his karate skills on one of the most popular T.V. shows at the time. This was one of the earliest exposures of karate on a large scale to the American public. This ad appeared in the **Hollywood Reporter**, one of the trade journals for the movie and T.V. industries, and according to Ed Parker it led to numerous Hollywood celebrities beginning to study karate.

Famous Isshin-ryu karate instructor Harold Long was one of the first Americans to teach karate in the Southwest. He was teaching in the early 1960s in Tennessee and became one of the U.S.K.A.'s best instructors. In 1975 with the permission of Isshin-ryu's founder Tatsuo Shimabuku, Long founded the International Isshin-Ryu Karate Association, and became its president.

**Aaron Banks** was one of the most prolific martial arts promoters in the United States, who staged over 500 events between 1967 and 1980. In 1967 he began the Oriental World of Self Defense, which exposed a large number of martial arts experts to the public. In 1974, Banks moved his event to Madison Square Gardens and drew almost 20,000 spectators – recording the highest paying live gate in the history of American Martial Arts. Banks was also the first to promote a major team contest in karate, as well as promoting the first Professional Karate Championships in 1968 at the Waldorf Astoria ballroom. It was here that Joe Lewis, Chuck Norris, Mike Stone and Skipper Mullins captured their world professional championship titles.

Hawaiian born Carlos Bunda (left), who won the lightweight division of the 1964 Long Beach International Karate Championships, was one of the first American karate champions.

The 1960s

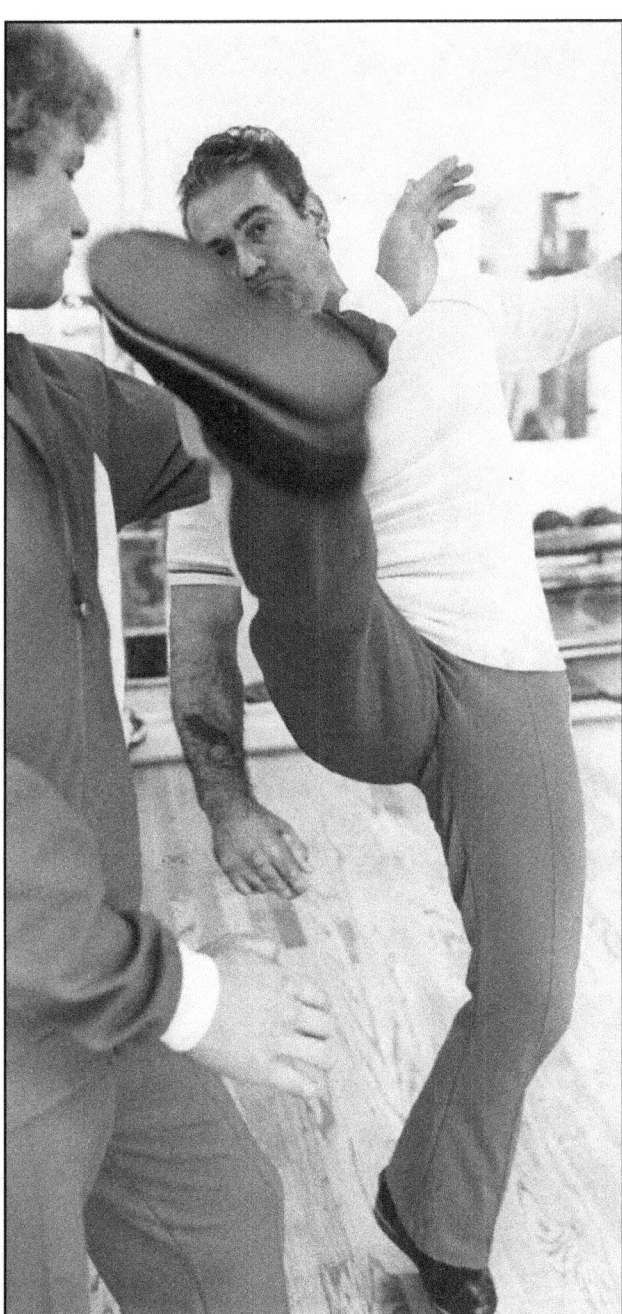

Don Buck was one of the first Americans to become a black belt in Mas Oyama's Kyokushinkai karate style. Living in San Francisco, Don taught karate for Oyama's organization until his death in 1998. Besides Kyokushinkai, Buck was also an expert in Hung gar kung fu.

Yoshiaki Ajari (right) is one of the most respected Japanese-American karate instructors in the United States. A Wado-ryu karate master, he came to the United States in 1957 and in 1960 he introduced Wado-Ryu to the United States. Living on the west coast, Ajari, is today, one of the world's foremost Wado-Ryu karate senseis.

Caylor Adkins (right) seen here with his sensei Tsutomu Oshima, was one of the first American karate instructors on the West Coast. He opened his own dojo in Long Beach in 1961 and has been teaching Shotokan karate ever since. A former AAU Karate Chairman, Adkins was responsible for organizing the 3rd WUKO World Karate Championships in 1975 in Long Beach.

An Illustrated History Of Martial Arts In America – 1900 to Present

Mito Uyehara (left) honoring Hayward Nishioka with a Black Belt Hall of Fame plaque. Uyehara, the founder and publisher of Black Belt Magazine, is one of the leading martial arts journalists in the world. The Hall of Fame was founded in 1968 to honor martial artists who's contribution to the arts have been great.

Below, at the 1996 East Coast Open Karate Tournament, some of the top Black Belts of the East Coast line up for a group shot.
  Left to right: Danny Pai, Harold Long, Ralph Linquist, Steve Armstrong, Ed McGrath, George Cofield, Don Nagel, Rus Kozuki, Thomas La Puppet, Joel Bucholz, Jerry Thomson, Pete Sirangano, Andrew Linick, and Ed Koludis.
*Courtesy of Gary Alexander*

Gary Alexander (center) was one of the earliest pioneers of karate in the United States. He established himself on the East Coast and was one of the earliest U.S. Karate Champions in the early 1960s. An Isshin-ryu stylist, he later became a leading instructor and tournament promoter. He is seen here with a young Louis Delgado (left) and Malachee Lee (right), both well-known champions in New York during the 1960s.

The 1960s

Washin-ryu karate instructor Hidy Ochai (Kneeling in black gi) had one of the largest karate schools in the United States during the 1960s. Located on the East Coast, Ochai became famous for his spectacular demonstrations and continued to be a leader of karate in the United States for many years He was also a top kata competitor during the 1970s.

Joo Bong Lee (above) is the supreme grand-master of the Korean martial art of hwarang do. A student of the fighting arts since childhood he taught his art in Korea, then in 1972 he emigrated to Southern California where he established the World Hwarang Do Association. Today, there are hundreds of schools teaching hwarang do in the U.S.

In the early days of American karate, before tournaments, inter-dojo matches were often held with two or three schools competing against each other. Here is a match held at an Isshin-ryu dojo in New Jersey during the early 1960s.  *Courtesy of Gary Alexander*

Taekwondo Master Jhoon Rhee is seen here wearing the 'Safe-T-Punch' and 'Safe-T- Kick' that he invented in the late 1960s. This foam-rubber protective gear revolutionized sport karate in the United States and overseas.

During the 1960s, many karate instructors tried to promote their art by demonstrations and exhibitions at public squares. Here, Gary Alexander and two of his black belts hold a demonstration on Wall Street.

An Illustrated History Of Martial Arts In America – 1900 to Present

A young Joe Lewis (center), seen here with Jhoon Rhee (left), and actor Robert Culp at the 1967 United States National Karate Championships, which Lewis won. Lewis went on to become one of America's greatest karate champions.

Ed Hamile was one of the earliest traditional karate instructors in Hawaii and was the first non-Japanese recipient of the Japan Karate Association's coveted Gichin Funakoshi Award. He was president of the JKA in Hawaii and his team was the first to defeat the Japanese team in kumite competition. In 1968, he founded the West Coast Shotokan Karate Association and became the Head of the Karate Referee Certification Program of the AAU. In 1994, he founded the World Federation of Karate Do Organizations.

In 1967, the first exchange practice took place between top American karate students and Japanese karate-ka from Waseda and Keio Universities. It was sponsored by Shotokan Master Tsutomu Oshima (left). Standing in the front line, are three American leading traditional karate champions (left to right) Caylor Adkins, John Gelson and Tony Tulleners.

The 1960s

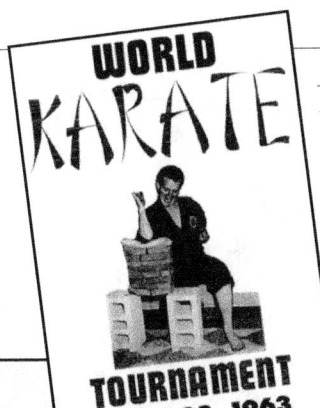

The poster advertising the First World Karate Tournament featured John Keehan demonstrating his breaking skills. The tournament sponsored by Keehan and Robert Trias was held at the University of Chicago Fieldhouse, and drew the leading American contestants and officials from around the country. This was the first truly national American karate tournament, and was won by Al Gene Carulla.

Some of the leading karate senseis who attended the 1st World Karate Tournament held in Chicago on July 28, 1963 included (left to right) Roy Oshiro, John Keehan, Phil Koeppel, George Mattson, Mas Tsuroka, Robert Trias, Ed Parker, Anthony Mirakian, Harold Long, Jhoon Rhee and Wendell Reeves.

One of the earliest and best known ju-jitsu instructors in the New York area was Antonio Pereira, who formed his own eclectic combat system called Miyamaryu-Jujutsu.

Shaolin kung fu Master, Ark-Yuey Wong, who moved to the United States in 1928, was the first sifu to teach his art openly to non-Asians at his Los Angeles kwoon. Before his death in 1987, Wong taught thousands of students classical kung fu, as well as weaponry. Besides his teaching skills he was also a well-respected herbalist.

# An Illustrated History Of Martial Arts In America – 1900 to Present

A self-defense course published in the early 1960s by body building guru Joe Weider. This was one of the best selling courses in the U.S. for many years.

The 1960s

Allen Steen (right), a student of Jhoon Rhee, was undoubtedly the most influential taekwondo instructor in the Southwestern United States. He opened his first commercial dojo in June of 1962, in Dallas, and became not only a superb instructor, but was one of America's legendary champions in the mid- and late-1960s. He was also a leading tournament promoter.

# KARATE
## JUDO - SAVATE
## JIU-JITSU

**THE GREATEST SELF-DEFENSE SYSTEM KNOWN TO MAN!**

When you complete our course—you may have the ability to break planks of wood in half—with your bare hands!!

Regardless of your age, you can master this TOTAL SELF-DEFENSE SYSTEM! It doesn't require muscles or size to be a MASTER at self-defense, but it does require KNOW-HOW!! The knowledge of Karate has enabled small, slight men to successfully and completely protect themselves from men twice their size; in just seconds the Karate Master can completely immobilize any attacker-destroying him. Easy to learn. Send TODAY for FREE COLORFUL BROCHURE!

Mail to:
UNIVERSAL
Dept. ZZ
Box 303
Detroit,
Mich. 48239

Name_____ Age___
Address_____
City_____
State_____ Zip_____

**FREE BROCHURE**

Ads like is became common during the 1960s.

Henry Cho was one of the earliest taekwondo instructors in the United States. He began teaching in New York in 1960 and soon had a large following. In 1965 he began the All-American Karate Championships which was one of the biggest tournaments in the United States at the time.

Two of New York's old time karate senseis were Chaka Zulu (right) and Ron Taganashi who was one of the founders of the Nisei Goju-ryu system. Taganashi was also well-known for his expertise in kobudo. Sensei Zulu was noted for his practical combat skills. He founded his own system of Zujitsu-ryu in 1984. *Courtesy of Beverly Hills Archives.*

An Illustrated History Of Martial Arts In America – 1900 to Present

In the 1960s, the All-American Karate Federation, founded by Hidetaka Nishiyama (left), became the largest traditional Japanese karate organization in the United States. The organization was mostly Shotokan-based.

San Francisco based Ralph Castro, who teaches his own Shaolin Kenpo Karate system, became famous not only for his teaching skills, but for producing a family of black belts, all of them seen here. Castro trained with William Chow and Ed Parker and began teaching in the early 1960s.

Roberta Trias (right) standing next to her father, Robert Trias, was one of the first well-known women karate black belts in the United States. She is seen here in the early 1960s. *Courtesy of R. Trias.*

The 1960s

Goju-ryu karate instructor Lou Angel is seen here with world famous Gogen Yamaguchi, with whom Angel studied. In 1961, Angel opened the "Institute of Karate" in Tulsa, which was the first dojo in Oklahoma. He later moved to Missouri and has continued to teach thousands of students over the years. Martial artist and actor Jeff Speakman is a protégé of Angel. *Courtesy of Lou Angel*

1967 Open Karate Championship held at the Manhattan Center. Back row (l-r) T. LaPuppet, L. Delgado, H. Lopez, R. Tagahashi, ?, J. Hess, ?, J. Hayes, A. Sternberg, ?, ?, ?, ?, R.Chun. Front row (l-r) L. Lee Cook, W. Swift, F. Edmunds, ?, T. Mason, ?.

James Wax is the father of the United States Matsubayashi Shorin-Ryu movement. While stationed in Okinawa with the marines, he trained under Ansei Ueshiro and, in 1961, he was hired to teach karate in Dayton and Cincinnati, Ohio, and in Indianapolis, Indiana. Most of the leading Shorin-Ryu karate instructors in the U.S. were his students, among them Bob Yarnall, Parker Shelton and Jim Harrison.

*Courtesy of W. Demetrich*

An Illustrated History Of Martial Arts In America – 1900 to Present

Bob Yarnall was a top competitor throughout the 1960s and was a leading member of the U.S.K.A under Robert Trias. He began teaching Shorin-ryu karate in the early '60s in the St. Louis area and has taught numerous well-known black belts including Parker Shelton.

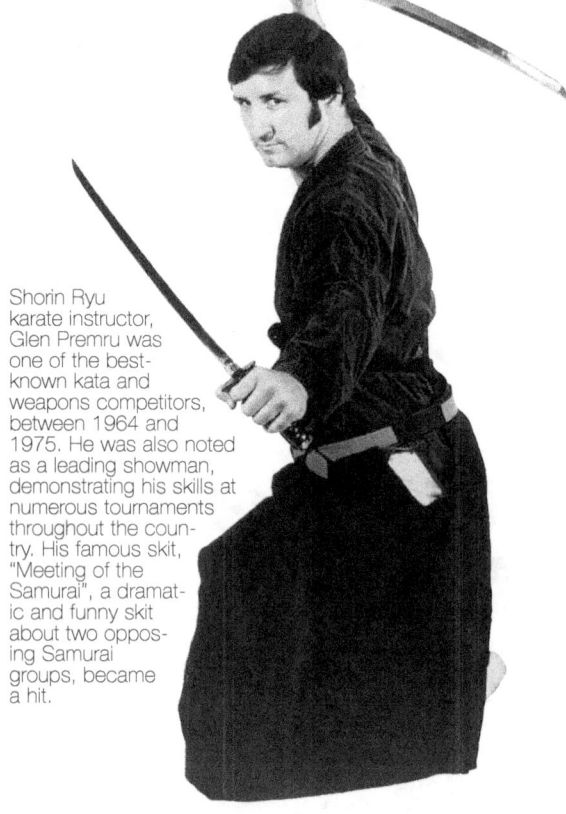

Shorin Ryu karate instructor, Glen Premru was one of the best-known kata and weapons competitors, between 1964 and 1975. He was also noted as a leading showman, demonstrating his skills at numerous tournaments throughout the country. His famous skit, "Meeting of the Samurai", a dramatic and funny skit about two opposing Samurai groups, became a hit.

Two of America's toughest fighters in the late 1960s and early 1970s were Fred Wren (left) and Skipper Mullins. Both fighters went on to become leading instructors that coached many regional and national champions.

Glenn Keeney (right) seen here delivering a kick to Bob Yarnall, was one of the USKA's top champions. In 1972-73 he was rated 4th among **Black Belt Magazine**'s Top Ten Competitors. A pioneer of Midwest karate, he was a well known official and trained a number of noted fighters, among them Ross Scott, a PKA full contact world champion.

The 1960s

Ed Parker was one of the earliest pioneers of karate in America. Located in Southern California, Parker, who founded the American Kenpo System, was one of the first karate experts to make appearances on television promoting his art. In 1964, he began The Long Beach International Karate Championships, which was, for many years, the most prestigious tournament in the country. He also was noted for teaching numerous Hollywood celebrities, including Elvis Presley.

Toyotaro Miyazaki (left) was a leading karate champion during the 1960s on the East Coast and is president of the United States Kenkyoku Karate Federation. In 1970, he was ranked 7th among the nation's top 10 fighters by **Black Belt Magazine**. Here, Miyazaki is competing at Tong Dojo Championships in 1968. Tom LaPuppet is the referee.

Anthony Mirakian, seen here (left) teaching a class was the first instructor to bring Okinawan Goju Ryu karate to American in 1960. Mirakian who trained in Okinawa under Meitoku Yagi, the foremost Goju master in Okinawa, continues to teach traditional Okinawan Meibukan Goju Ryu in its purest form.

New York's Fred Miller was one of the earliest karate champions on the East Coast. He's seen here in the white gi at a local tournament with Aaron Banks refereeing. Miller later became a light-heavyweight full contact karate champion with the World Professional Karate Organization.

The 1st Canadian Karate-Do Open Championships was sponsored by Mas Tsuroka and held in Toronto, Ontario. It was one of the first large "Open" karate tournaments held in North America, and many top American and Canadian fighters participated in the event, which was won by famous East Coast Isshin-Ryu black belt Gary Alexander.

Chuck Sereff is one of the leading Taekwondo instructors in the United States. In 1963, he opened the first Korean style martial arts academy in Denver, Colorado. In 1974, he founded the United States Taekwondo Federation (USTF). He has coached numerous American teams that have competed in the International Taekwondo Federation World Championships. *Courtesy of C. Sereff*

Allen Steen (top row right) seen with his first karate class in 1962. *Courtesy of K. Yates*

## The 1960s

William Dometrich refereeing a typical dojo tournament at his school in 1962.

Al Gene Carulia (with trophies) was the winner at the 1st World Karate Championships held in Chicago in 1963. This was the first really big American Karate Tournament. In the photo to the right of Carulia is John Keehan, one of the tournament's sponsors. Fourth from the left is Robert Trias, the other sponsor of the tournament. Second from the left is Phil Koeppel.

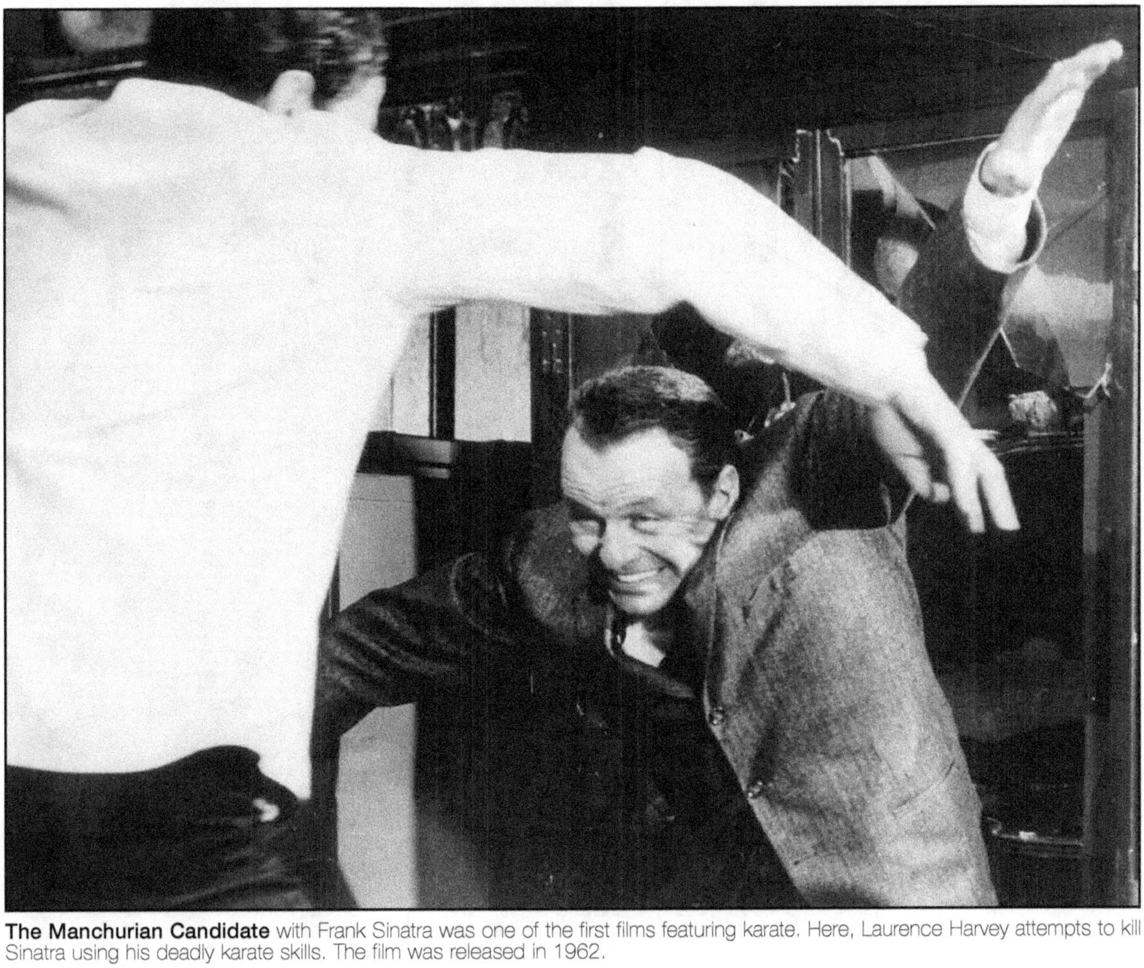

**The Manchurian Candidate** with Frank Sinatra was one of the first films featuring karate. Here, Laurence Harvey attempts to kill Sinatra using his deadly karate skills. The film was released in 1962.

Canadian Chito-ryu competitor Shane Higashi (left) defeats America's Sam Pearson at the 1963 Canadian Karate Championships. Referee is John Keehan.

Bruce Lee's first book was published in 1963 before he became a Hollywood celebrity. At just under one hundred pages, it was one of the first English language books on the subject.

Three of Shotokan's top competitors at the 1963 All American Karate Championships. 1st place: James Yabe, 2nd place: Ken Funakoshi, and 3rd place: Ray Dalke. Yabe won this event in 1961, '62, '63, '66 and '67. Today, all three men are among the highest ranking Shotokan practitioners in the U.S.

The 1960s

In the early 1960s, Ed Parker was one of the few karate instructors who worked on television and gave lessons to well-known stars of the time. Here he is with Lucille Ball and Vivian Vance in an episode of **The Lucy Show** entitled *Lucy and Viv Learn Judo*. It was aired on February 25, 1963, on CBS. *Courtesy of E. Parker*

Bruce Lee poses with Ed Parker (left) and leading karate sensei Bill Ryusaki at Parker's 1964 Long Beach Karate Tournament. It was at this event that Lee was discovered by Hollywood when he demonstrated his incredible skills. This eventually led him to the role of Kato in **The Green Hornet** T.V. series.

Mas Tsuroka's 2nd Canadian Championships in 1963 drew some of the best-known black belts in North America. Front row (l-r): Russell Benefeil, Roland Albarado, Sam Pearson, Phil Koeppel, Mas Tsuroka, Harry Smith, James Cheetham, John Keehan. Second row: William Dometrich, Russ Hank, Ralph Lindquest, ?, ?, ?, Jim McLean, ? ,? , Back row (second from left): Pete Mussachio, (fourth from left) Robin Rielly, (last on right) Shane Higashi (winner of the event).

# An Illustrated History Of Martial Arts In America – 1900 to Present

Sam Pearson (right) was one of the early pioneers of karate in the United States. He was a Shorin-ryu karate instructor and was a top competitor in the early 1960s. He is seen here after winning a karate tournament in 1964 at Camp Lejune, North Carolina. At left is Donald Bohan, another early karate champion.

In 1964, at Ed Parker's Internationals, the American public got their first exposure to Bruce Lee, who put on a spectacular demonstration. His demonstration included his famous "one inch punch" in which Lee held his fists one inch from the opponent's chest and drove him back into a chair. Lee's demo led him to land the role of "Kato" in **The Green Hornet** T.V. series.

In April of 1964, Chuck Norris (left) takes home the trophies for fighting and kata at the Orange County Karate Tournament. This was one of Norris' first tournaments. Next to Norris is runner-up Kenny Osborne.  *Courtesy of B. Wall*

In 1964, Isao Obato founded the American Society of Classical Judo-ka (ASCT). The organization's objective was to organize and promote judo as a martial art and not as a sport.

The 1960s

**The Karate Dojo** by Peter Urban, was originally published in 1964. It was later re-published in 1967 by Tuttle. It was the first book by an American karate sensei to cover the culture, philosophy and traditions of the art and became a bestseller.

Some of America's top Judo competitors of the 1960s, with the 1964 Olympic coach, Yoshihiro Uchida; (l-r): George Harris, Jim Bregman, Yosh Uchida, Paul Maruyama and Ben Campbell. This was the American judo team that represented the U.S. at the 1964 Olympics.

A 1964 ad for Bruce Lee's school in Oakland.

In the summer of 1964, Ed Parker promoted the 1st International Karate Championships in the Long Beach Auditorium. This was the first truly large open karate tournament in the United States. Within years, a number of promoters were copying Parker's event, but Parker's tournament for many years was the most prestigious in the country, with almost every major star competing. The tournament was also noted for its incredible demonstrations performed by many of the greatest martial artists in America, including the first appearance by Bruce Lee at the 1964 event.

An Illustrated History Of Martial Arts In America – 1900 to Present

One of the earliest and largest karate tournaments in North America was held in Toronto in 1964. Sponsored by Mas Tsuroka, the Canadian International Open Championships drew competitors from all over the world. Among the leading American competitors seen here are (front row, l-r) Artis Simmons (2nd), Tom LaPuppet (3rd), Ralph Lindquist (5th), and William Dometrich (6th).

Director and writer Blake Edwards a karate student of Ed Parkers, gets Peter Sellers (left) to spoof the martial arts in the comedy feature A Shot in the Dark. The film was released in 1964.

The 1960s

At the 1965 AAU US National Judo Championships, Risei Kano, son of Jigoro Kano, awards Hayward Nishioka the grand championship silver cup. Nishioka also won the event in '66 and '70 and went on to become one of the leaders of judo in the US and has written extensively on the subject.

John Pachivas, who began teaching karate in the 1950s, is noted as the "Father of Karate in Florida". One of the leading members of the United States Karate Association, Pachivas was the highest ranking person in Shuri-ryu karate-do (10th dan) when he passed away in 2000.

In 1966, Sea Oh Choi (throwing an opponent) brought Hapkido to the United States. He opened a dojo in Los Angeles, but the art remained relatively unknown until 1972 when it was used in the film **Billy Jack**.

Fumio Demura (kicking), who introduced Chito-ryu karate here, was an All-Japan Karate Champion when he came to teach in the United States in 1965. *Courtesy of F. Demura*

In December of 1965, the first official international karate match was held between a U.S. team and the All-Japan Collegiate Karate Team, who are seen here arriving in San Francisco where the event took place. Hidetaka Nishiyama (4th from the left) was the coach for the American team. The result was 3 to 1 in favor of the Japanese team with one draw.

# An Illustrated History Of Martial Arts In America – 1900 to Present

The "Father of Escrima in America" Angel Cabales (left) began his training at an early age and became a sailor, finally settling in the United States in Stockton, California. There, in 1966, he opened the first public Filipino martial arts academy in the United States and taught there for over a quarter of a century. Cabales has instructed thousands of students from all over the world, many who became leading instructors. He passed away in 1991.

George Pesare (right) with one of his black belts, Nick Cerio, introduced Kempo karate to Rhode Island in 1961. Over the years, he has produced a large number of well-known karate champions and instructors. He promoted Rhode Island's first karate tournament in 1966 and became one of the best-known instructors on the East Coast.

Sensei Fumio Demura was the man most responsible for the introduction of kobudo (martial arts weaponry) into the U.S. when he began giving demos with nunchaku, sai and bo during the mid-1960s. He was also the first to author books using many of these weapons.

Sifu Paul Eng is one of the top kung fu instructors in America. He moved to the U.S. in 1949 and, in 1959, became chief instructor of the Fu Jow Pai Kung fu Federation. In 1965, he relocated to Northern California and specialized in teaching the Praying Mantis style. He is presently head of the Tai Mantis Kung fu Association.

The 1960s

In the early 1960s, Bruce Tegner (left) and his sister were frequent guests on various T.V. shows demonstrating and promoting the martial arts. Here they are with famous T.V. host Art Linklater, who looks a bit surprised after being tossed over by Tegner.

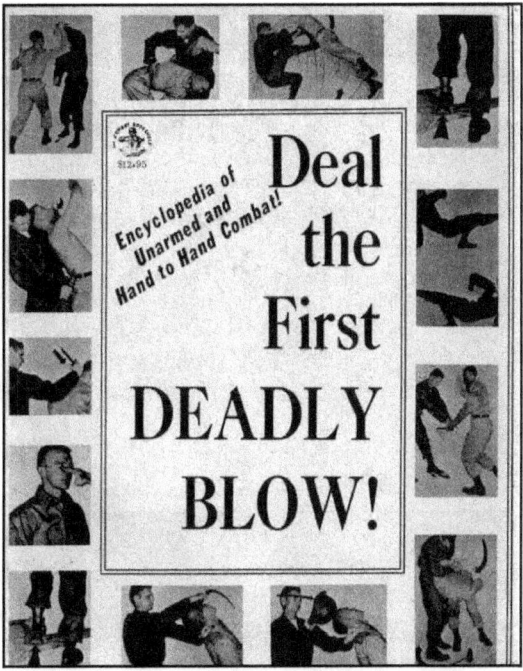

Published in the early '60s this 330-page book was the most comprehensive book on military-style self defense for the laymen.

Taekwondo expert Kang Rhee was a leading taekwondo practitioner in Korea before moving to the United States in 1964. He established the Pa Sa Ryu Mu Do Association in Memphis, Tennessee in 1966 and became a leading instructor in the area. Among his most famous students was Elvis Presley.

Shito-ryu karate sensei Minobu Miki (kicking), who moved to the United States in 1966, besides becoming a top competitor he also became one of the most respected traditional instructors in the U.S.A. A highly respected referee, Miki makes his headquarters in San Diego.

Bob White (right) is one of the leading Kempo instructors in the United States. A student of Ed Parker's since 1966, White was a consistent winner at numerous tournaments. Since 1972, when he opened his first dojo in Southern California, he has produced numerous top competitors.

One of the earliest female black belts on the East Coast who specialized in teaching women's self-defense was Bonnie Baker Taganashi, wife of famous karate champion Ron Taganashi. *Courtesy of R. Taganashi*

Judo champion Gene Le Bell was a top Hollywood stuntman who took thousands of falls for numerous major stars. Here he is about to be thrown by Elvis Presley. *Courtesy of Gene LeBell*

The 1960s

Jimmy Jones was one of the top karate fighters from Chicago during the 1960s. He became chief instructor in Chicago for the U.S.K.A and became one of the best-known karate sensei in the Midwest, teaching the likes of Ken Knudson.

Jules Paulin of the Philadelphia Karate Club was one of the earliest East Coast Shotokan champions. He won numerous traditional tournaments during the mid-1960s, including the prestigious All America Karate Federation Championships and East Coast karate Championships.

The **Green Hornet** T.V. series, starring Van Williams (right) introduced Bruce Lee to American audiences in the role of Kato. Although the show only lasted for one season (1966-67), it was instrumental in promoting martial arts throughout the country and was partially responsible for the huge martial arts craze that soon followed. In almost every episode, Lee got to show off his incredible martial arts skills and it was the beginning of his future stardom.     *Courtesy of 20th Century Fox T.V.*

An Illustrated History Of Martial Arts In America – 1900 to Present

Frank Smith (left) was among the top Shotokan competitors in the United States during the 1960s. A student of Hidetaka Nishiyama, Smith was considered by many to be the toughest fighter in the United States during his competitive years.

Kyokushinkai karate master Mas Oyama (center) is flanked by two of his top black belts: Tadashi Nakamura (left) and Shigeru Oyama. Nakamura moved to the U.S. in 1966 and ten years later founded the World Seido Karate Organization with headquarters in New York. Shigeru Oyama moved here in 1965 and founded his own World Oyama Organization in 1985.

Karate champions Joe Lewis (left) and Bob Wall teach karate to a group of playboy bunnies at their Sherman Oaks dojo in the mid-1960s.

# The 1960s

Moses Powell was one of the best-known martial arts instructors in New York during the 1960's and 1970's. He was a renowned performer and was a regular demonstrator at New York's World Fair in 1965. He taught his own Sanuce ju-jitsu style and was the first African American martial artist to teach the FBI and Secret Service. He taught for over 40 years and passed away on January 22, 2005.
*Courtesy of R. Van Clief.*

Two of the East Coast's leading taekwondo senseis, Richard Chun (Left) and Ki Whang Kim (right), are seen here in the mid-1960s with three East Coast champions (l-r): Hector Eugui, Mitchell Bobrow, and Joe Hayes.

*Courtesy of Mitchell Bobrow*

Two superstars of American Karate were Chuck Norris (right) and Ron Marchini. Here they are competing at a California tournament in the mid-1960s. *Courtesy of Beverly Hills Archives*

By the mid-1960s, women were beginning to seek out karate classes in order to learn self-defense. Lillian Wall, wife of Bob Wall, is shown here at the far right. Circa 1965 - Sherman Oaks Karate.

Early East Coast karate pioneers are seen at a New York tournament during the mid-1960s. Left to right: Ed Kaloudis, Andrew Linick, Lou Lizzote and Tom LaPuppet. *Courtesy of Beverly Hills Archives*

An Illustrated History Of Martial Arts In America – 1900 to Present

By the mid-1960s, ads like these, in which martial arts and martial artists were used to promote various items, were becoming common.

One of the most often seen ads in the late 1960s was this one, which promoted Dim Mak – the "Death Touch" – by Count Dante (really John Keehan, a Chicago based karate black belt).

Nunchakus became popular in the 1960s and ads like this were common.

The 1960s

During the 1960's, John Davis a New York based martial artist was one of the top competitors and demonstrators. His incredible showmanship was unique and promoters sought him out regularly. Courtesy of R. Van Clief.

James Coburn portrayed a James Bond spin off in the movie **Our Man Flint**. Trained personally by Bruce Lee, Coburn shows off his martial arts skills in the movie, which was released in 1966. Coburn became one of Lee's closest friends and was instrumental in introducing him to Hollywood.

Shotokan karate expert Thomas La Puppet was the first East Coast karate champion to gain national fame on the American tournament circuit during the mid to late 1960's. A student of George Cofield's, La Puppet after 1970 became a top instructor and later became involved in the AAU karate program and worked tirelessly to get karate into the Olympics. He passed away in 1999. Courtesy of R. Van Clief.

John Keehan (left) seen here with his student, Al Gene Caraulia, was one of the earliest karate instructors in Chicago. A student of Robert Trias, Keehan a prolific promoter, was often involved in controversy and, in the mid-1970s, an altercation with another dojo led to the death of black belt, Jim Kohcevic. Keehan who also assumed the name of "Count Dante" became well known for his self-promotion as the "Deadliest Man Alive." He passed away in 1975. *Courtesy of J. Jones*

Ernest Lieb, who got his black belt in karate at age 18, founded the American Karate Association in 1964 after he returned from Korea, where he served in the air force. Settling in Muskegon, Michigan, he began teaching the "American Karate System," a blend of numerous styles. During the mid- to late-1960s, he was one of the top competitors in the Mid West, and since 1964, he has been one of the best known and most respected instructors in his area, producing numerous well-known black belts. *Courtesy of E. Lieb*

Shorin-ryu karate expert Sid Campbell is one of the leading senseis in Northern California. He began teaching in Oakland in 1967 and has taught ever since. He is an expert in Okinawan Kobudo and has written numerous books on the various martial arts.

Bruce Lee (left) congratulates Joe Lewis for winning Jhoon Rhee's United National Karate Championships in 1967 in Washington, D.C. *Courtesy of Joe Lewis*

In the mid-1960s, Hollywood-based sensei Tak Kubota was one of the few traditional instructors who invited numerous open style karate champions to his events. He came to the U.S. in 1965 and became one of the most respected Japanese senseis in the country. Here, he is shaking hands with Chuck Norris, winner of one of his tournaments. Next to Norris is karate champion Ron Marchini. *Courtesy of Beverly Hills Archive*

The 1960s

In the 1960s, two of the top Shotokan karate champions in America were Frank Smith (right) and Kenneth Funakoshi. They are seen here at the 1967 All America Karate Championships.

Al Weiss was the founder and publisher of **Official Karate Magazine** in 1968. The New York based magazine was, for many years, one of the leading martial arts publications in the United States. Weiss was a black belt under John Kuhl and became one of the most influential martial artists on the East Coast. *Courtesy of David Weiss*

Two of America's greatest karate champions, Joe Lewis (left) and Chuck Norris, face off at the 1967 Long Beach Internationals. The referee is Steve Armstrong. *Courtesy of Beverly Hills Archives*

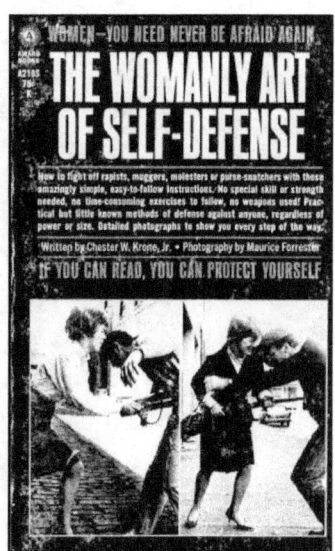

One of the earliest pocket books on Women's Self Defense was this one, which appeared in 1967.

An Illustrated History Of Martial Arts In America – 1900 to Present

A group of leading American karate instructors around 1968, from left to right: Bob Yarnall, Jim McClain, John Kennedy, John Pachivas, Phil Koeppel, Jim Champman and Jimmy Jones. *Courtesy of M. Townsley*

Park Jong Soo opened the first taekwondo schools in Canada in 1968, in Toronto. A student of General Choi Hong Hi, Soo has traveled worldwide promoting Taekwondo in the mid-1960s and was instrumental in the art's growth.

Sean Connery visits a Ninja training center in the 1967 James Bond adventure film, **You Only Live Twice**. This was the first major motion picture to prominently feature ninjas.

Jae Chul Shin is one of the leading Korean Tang Soo Do instructors. He moved to the U.S. in 1968 and settled in Burlington, New Jersey. That same year he formed the United States Tang Soo Do Federation and has been instrumental in promoting the art worldwide. In 1982, he founded the World Tang Soo Do Association.

The 1960s

Grandmaster Leo Giron, known as the father of Largo Mano in America, was one of the most influential Filipino martial arts instructors in the U.S. He moved to California in 1926, became a WWII veteran and opened his first school the Baha na club in 1968. From 1970 on, he lived and taught in Stockton, where he taught some of the top martial artists such as Danny Inosanto, Dentoy Revilar, Richard Bustillo and Ted Lucay Lucay. He passed away in 2002 at the age of 91.

A group of early East Coast Karate pioneers c. 1968 Top (l-r): Frank Ruiz, Chaka Zulu, Alex Sternberg, ?, Malakai Lee, Tomas La Puppet, Sgt. Joe Henry, ?, Andrew Linnick. Bottom: Owen Watson, Ron Taganashi, ?.

Bob Wall (left) and Chuck Norris became partners in 1968 when Norris bought out Joe Lewis's share in the Sherman Oaks Karate School, which was originally opened by Wall and Lewis in 1966. Norris and Wall expanded the one school into a successful chain of karate schools. *Courtesy of B. Wall*

On June 14, 1968, the Japanese government presented judo Master Toshitaka Yamauchi with 'The Order of Sacred Treasure Medal' for his contribution to the sport of judo in the United States. Yamauchi, who came to the United States in 1917, settled in the Los Angeles area and was instrumental in helping the formation of numerous dojos across the United States.

An Illustrated History Of Martial Arts In America – 1900 to Present

This was the first martial arts convention held in the U.S. It was sponsored by **Black Belt Magazine** and visited by leading martial artists from all over the country. They came to exchange ideas and discuss the state and future of the martial arts in America.

Glenn Keeney (right) one of the midwest's top fighters gets scored on by Joe Corley.

Ryobu-kan karate master Kiyoshi Yamazaki who moved to the United States in 1969 is also an expert in Iaido. He was the sword instructor to Arnold Schwarzenegger in the film **Conan The Barbarian** (1982). Yamazaki sensei overseas all of the schools of the Japan Karate Do Ryobukai and is a member of the World Karate Federation's technical committee. He is one of the most respected traditional martial arts instructors in the United States.

Katsutaka Tanaka (right) is a former Japanese karate champion who opened a dojo in Anchorage, Alaska, in 1969 where he teaches Shito-ryu karate and Kobudo. He is one of the most respected senseis in the United States and, since 1973, has promoted the "Top of the World Karate Championships" the largest in Alaska.

Kenneth Kuniyuki, American Judo pioneer, was born in Seattle and, in 1932, traveled to Japan to further his judo training. He moved to Los Angeles in the mid-1930s and became a leading figure in Southern California judo, helping to produce numerous champions. He was instrumental in creating the U.S. Judo Federation (formerly the Judo Black Belt Federation) and became its first president. He passed away in 2002 at age 92.

The 1960s

Dirk Mosig (right) was a top U.S.K.A. fighter and instructor during the late 1960s. He was voted "best tournament coach" in 1969 by the U.S.K.A. *Courtesy of M. Townsley*

Published in 1969, this book by Donn Draeger and Robert W. Smith, was the first to explore in depth the history of the Asian martial arts.

Noted for his incredible kicking skills, Texan Skipper Mullins (right) was consistently rated among the top 10 fighters in the United States during the late 1960s and early 1970s. He is one of the legends of American sport karate and became a noted instructor after his retirement. He is seen here attacking famous U.S. champion Ron Marchini.

Pat Worley (left) defeats James Stevens in Dallas, Texas, at the 1969 United States Open. Referee is Chuck Norris. *Courtesy of Pat Worley*

An Illustrated History Of Martial Arts In America – 1900 to Present

The Certificate of Achievement given to Steve McQueen by his instructor, Bruce Lee.

Among the best-known Hollywood celebrity to study with Bruce Lee was Steve McQueen (left). He began training with Lee in the late 1960s.

Alex Sternberg is a leading Shotokan karate instructor in the New York area. A student of George Cofield, Sternberg was a top kata competitor in the late 1960s and early 1970s. Since retiring from competition, he has produced a number of top American karate competitors. Currently he promotes a yearly traditional karate tournament called the "Big Apple Challenge."

Academy award winning screenwriter (**Heat of the Night**, 1968) Stirling Silliphanat was a great martial arts enthusiast. He was a personal friend and private student of Bruce Lee's and was responsible for putting Lee into the **Longstreet** T.V. series in 1971, as well as into the film **Marlowe** with James Garner in 1969.

In the late 1960s, kung fu master Pui Chan introduced the Wah Lum kung fu system to the U.S. One of the most respected Sifus in America, Chan in 1980 built a kung fu temple in Orlando – the "Wah Lum Temple" – where he allows instructors from all over the country to live and undertake intensive training.

George Cofield was one of New York's best-known Shotokan karate instructors. During the 1960s and 1970s, students at his famous Tong dojo were unbeatable and he produced dozens of top champions, including Thomas La Puppet and Alex Sternberg. *Courtesy of R. Van Clief*

Tino Tuiolosega, a Samoan martial arts instructor, formed the Lima Lama fighting system based on numerous Hawaiian arts. He moved to Southern California where, from the late 1960s, he founded a large organization and became one its major figureheads. He produced a number of well-known black belts.

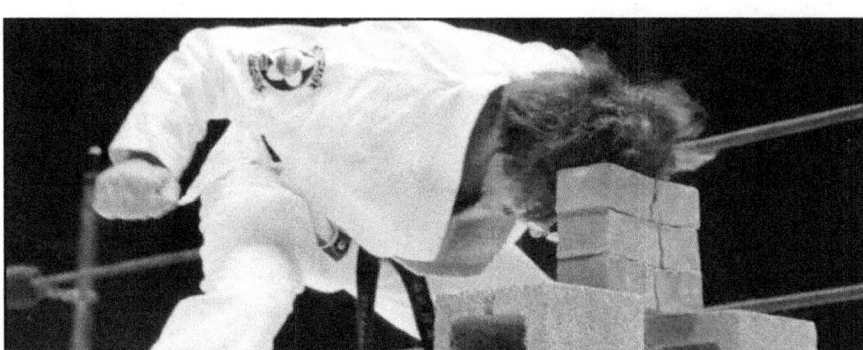

A head break by Koeikan karate pioneer, Ed Kaloudis, at Madison Square Gardens' Oriental World of Self Defense. This event, promoted by Aaron Banks, gave many East Coast senseis national exposure via television. Kaloudis was the first sensei to teach karate on the East Coast, beginning in 1954.
*Courtesy of Ed Kaloudis*

John Gehlsen, seen here defeating an unknown opponent, was one of Tak Kubota's top students and was one of the best traditional karate fighters in the U.S. during the late 1960s. Many considered him to be one of the toughest fighters in karate.

Jim Harrison is one of the pioneers of karate in Kansas and is one of the mid-west's best-known instructors. A former judo and karate champion during the late 1960s, Harrison was one of the toughest fighters ever to step into the karate ring. He staged the first professional karate tournament in the U.S. in Kansas City, Missouri, in 1968.

The 1960s

Okinawa Goju-ryu karate sensei Teruo Chinen, who moved to the U.S. in 1969, has become one of the leading karate senseis in the U.S. He is headquartered in Spokane, Washington, from where he runs his Jundokan International, an organization with affiliates worldwide.

Donnie Williams (right) was a leading West Coast martial arts instructor and competitor during the 1970s, and was one of the co-founders of the Black Karate Federation in the late 1960s. Originally a taekwondo stylist, he later became a student of Steve Mohammed (Steve Sanders). Today, he is an ordained minister with a congregation in Southern California.

Presentation of awards at Jhoon Rhee's first National Karate Championships in 1964 in Washington, D.C., which was, for many years, the most prestigious tournament on the East Coast. Standing (l-r): Zenpo Shimabuku, Anthony Mirakian, Jhoon Rhee, Ed Parker, Mike Stone, General Curtis LeMay (honored guest), and Joseph Pennywell. Seated is grand champion Pat Burleson.  *Courtesy of A. Mirakian*

An Illustrated History Of Martial Arts In America – 1900 to Present

Allen Steen (right) faces of against Chuck Norris at the 1966 Long Beach internationals, where Steen won the grand championships and Norris captured the middleweight title.

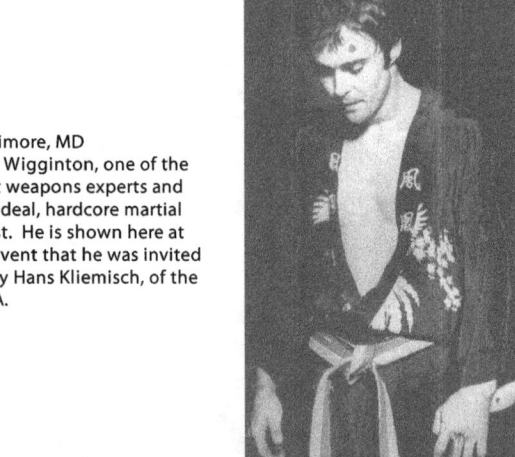

Baltimore, MD
Rick Wigginton, one of the best weapons experts and real deal, hardcore martial artist. He is shown here at an event that he was invited to by Hans Kliemisch, of the IKKA.

Texas karate champion Pat Burleson was one of the earliest big name karate competitors in the U.S., beginning with victories in 1962. Noted for his 'rough and tumble' brand of karate, he was known as the "grandfather" of open tournament fighting in America. Burleson had a major impact on the growth of karate in the Southwest and many of his students became well known champions. Burleson (r) is seen here fighting Mike Stone in 1965. *Courtesy of P. Burleson*

Mitchell Bobrow, a student of Ki Whang Kim, received his black belt in 1965 and in the following years he became one of America's top champions. Known as the "Boy Wonder", Bobrow was noted for his superb kicks, and he fought and defeated many of the leading champions at the time. Today, he runs Otomix, a martial arts gear company. *Courtesy of M. Bobrow*

# The 1960s

Donn Draeger was regarded as the foremost Western scholar of the Japanese martial arts. A former marine, Draeger who lived all over Asia began his training with judo, and was instrumental in establishing the sport in the U.S. He later authored numerous bestselling books an all areas of the arts, including **Asian Fighting Arts** which is a classic. He is seen here in 1967 teaching Sean Connery the use of the bo for the James Bond film **You Only live Twice**. *Courtesy of Beverly Hills Archives*

**Judo Master** appeared in 1966 and helped promote the influx of children into judo schools.

Some of the leaders of American karate are seen here at the first Long Beach International Karate Championships in 1964. Front row (l-r): Pat Burleson, Bruce Lee, Anthony Mirakian, Jhoon Rhee. Back row (l-r): Allen Steen, George Mattson, Ed Parker, Tatsuo Oshima, Robert Trias. *Courtesy of A. Mirakian*

Kenneth Funakoshi is one of the top Shotokan karate instructors in the U.S. Originally from Hawaii, he studied karate under some of Japan's leading senseis and was grand champion of the prestigious Karate Association of Hawaii Tournament from 1964-1968. In 1968 he moved to San Jose where he founded the Funakoshi Shotokan Karate Association with affiliates worldwide.

Arlene Francis played a private detective who was a judo expert on the A.B.C. television series **Honey West**, which aired in 1965-66. Here, Francis is seen throwing famous judo legend Gene LeBell.

American karate pioneer Steve Armstrong (left) began his martial arts training in the Orient and became one of Tatsuo Shimabuku's top students. He began teaching Isshin-ryu karate in the early early 1960s in Tacoma, Washington, and became one of the country's most respected instructors. He was also one of the most highly-regarded karate referees during the early days of American karate.

An Illustrated History Of Martial Arts In America – 1900 to Present

Hal Sharp, shown with two of his best-selling books, is one of the most knowledgeable American judo instructors in the U.S. Sharp, who lived in Japan for years, trained with some of the greatest judo masters in the world and began teaching in Southern California in the early 1960s.

Famous Hollywood author Joe Hyams is seen here in an early ad for Ed Parker's Kenpo Karate Schools. Hyams, who had studied martial arts with some of the countries leading masters, was one of Bruce Lee's first private students and it was through Hyams that Lee got to meet many of Hollywood's top luminaries. In 1979 Hyams wrote the best-selling book, **Zen and the Martial Arts**.

Robert W. Smith is one of America's leading martial arts historians and authors. He was one of the first Americans to study the Chinese internal martial arts while living in Taiwan, and was instrumental in introducing these arts to Americans through his numerous books on the subject. He has authored over a dozen books, including under the pseudonym of John Gilbey, and co-authored the classic **Asian Fighting Arts** with Don Draeger in 1969.

Mike Stone (center) accepts the first place trophy from Ed Parker (right) and famous film producer-director Blake Edwards at the first Long Beach Internationals held in 1964. Stone went on to an impressive record of 91 undefeated matches, becoming one of the earliest stars of American sport karate.

Richard Reed was one of the first Americans to teach Taekwondo in the U.S. He trained in Korea under Haeng Ung Lee and in 1962 opened a school in Tacoma, Washington. He bought master Lee to the U.S. and in 1966 they formed an organization that eventually became the American Taekwondo Association (ATA) the biggest Korean organization in the U.S.

The 1960s

**Official Karate** magazine was the first East Coast martial arts publication, created by Al Weiss in 1968. Featured on this cover is William Louie.

Mike Foster was one of the first karate instructors in Florida. A Yoshinkai stylist, he was a top Southern competitor in the '60s and '70s, and was one of the first to teach an accredited karate course at an American university

Richard Kim was one of the best known martial artists in the U.S. and was noted as the foremost martial arts historian in the country. He began his training in the mid-1920s and came to the U.S. in 1959, settling in San Francisco where he began to teach karate and kobudo to thousands of students. He wrote a number of books, including the best-selling, **Weaponless Warrior**, and had hundreds of articles published worldwide. He passed away in 2001.

An Illustrated History Of Martial Arts In America – 1900 to Present

Ninjas were first exposed to the American martial arts community in December of 1966 when **Black Belt Magazine** featured these "invisible warriors" on it's cover. It wasn't till the early 1980s that the "ninja craze" hit America. *Courtesy of Black Belt Magazine*

In the mid 1960s, 8mm. martial arts instructional film was becoming popular. It would be another fifteen years before the video market made film obsolete.

Officials and competitors at the first Northern vs. Southern California Karate Tournament in 1962. Behind barrier (l-r): Yoshiaki Ajari, Gosen Yamaguchi, Richard Kim, Hidetaka Nishiyama, Walter Todd and Duke Moore. Standing in gis (l-r): ?,?,?, Ray Dalke, ?, Takashi Aoki, ?, James Yabe, Caylor Atkins, John Pereira, Leroy Rodriguez, Jerry Streeter, George Kuwamoto, Clarence Lee, Richard Lee, Vince Cuoco, and Frank Yuen. These yearly events were started by Moore and Nishiyama and continued for over twenty years.

# The 1970s

    This was the decade that Americans discovered kung-fu, and the movies discovered the martial arts. Karate was still king, but thanks mostly to the movies from Hong Kong, kung-fu began to be widely taught, though often by bogus experts. Taekwondo came to the forefront of martial arts. Hundreds of Korean masters emigrated to the U.S. and by the end of the '70s Korean karate was the mostly widely practiced martial art.
    Bruce Lee became a legend and his film **Enter the Dragon** bought him stardom, though sadly he died the same year the film was released in 1973. Thanks to the movies, the martial arts grew substantially. In the early '70s, as films used more and more martial arts type action in their fight sequences, stunt coordinators were hiring black belts to act as fight directors while Hollywood producers financed martial arts movies.
    By the mid 1970s, full contact karate was introduced into the U.S. Unlike its traditional cousin, where combatants pulled their punches and kicks, full contact fighters went for the knockout. Many claimed that due to full contact, the enrollment in dojos began to decline. It wasn't until the end of the decade that the martial arts boom again took place.

## An Illustrated History Of Martial Arts In America – 1900 to Present

Erik Lee, known as the "Little King of Kata", was among the top competitors during the early 1970s.

An expert in Chinese kung fu, he was also famous for his expertise with numerous Chinese weapons, including the double sword, spear, steel whip and the three sectional staff.

After retiring from competition, Lee was constantly in demand as a demonstrator at tournaments and various martial arts events. He later got involved in working in movies.

Jerry Smith is the co-founder of the Black Karate Federation. He was the captain of the BKF team that won the Long Beach International Karate Championships three times in a row 1971, 72, 73. He was one of the first full contact karate coaches in the United States.

Andrew Linick is a well-known East Coast martial artist who was a top regional competitor and is an expert in Okinawan kobudo. He authored a number of books and has been a pioneer in introducing martial arts courses into public schools and colleges.

# The 1970s

Al Dacascos was one of the first kung fu experts to compete successfully at American karate tournaments. He was a consistent winner in both sparring and kata in the late 1960s and early 1970s. A former student of Kajukenbo master Adriano Emperado, Dacascos founded his own style, Wun Hop Kuen Do (the way of the combined fist) in 1969. Over the years, he has produced a number of notable students, including his son Mark, Malia Bernel, Karen Shepherd, Bill Owens and Eric Lee.

Joe Hayes (left) seen here at a tournament in Washington, D.C., was one of the top American karate competitors during the late 1960s and 1970s. He was captain of the American team that placed second in the 1st World Taekwondo Championships in 1973. He won the bronze medal at the same event. Noted for his reverse punch and multiple aerial kicks, Hayes was one of the most spectacular fighters on the American karate circuit.

"The King" Elvis Aaron Presley, 7th dan black belt, in a Memphis, Tennessee dojo.

Two of America's premier karate competitors, Bill Wallace (in black) and Roy Kurban battle it out during the days of semi-contact karate in the early 1970s.

An Illustrated History Of Martial Arts In America – 1900 to Present

American Karate superstar Chuck Norris (right) fights against Arnold Urquidez, whose brother Benny, under Arnold's coaching, became the greatest American full contact karate champion in the 1980s. The referee seen here in the white gi is Jim Harrison.

Karyn Turner (kneeling) was the founder of the Hard Knocks, the first professional martial arts demo team in the United States. Between 1970 and 1975 they performed at most major karate events and held performances in Las Vegas and Lake Tahoe. They even had a special on ABC. Turner, a student of Al Dacascos, was a number one kata competitor in the United States during the 1970s.

Vincent Marchetti was one of the pioneers of martial arts in the New York area. He teaches Michi Budo Ryu which combines judo, ju-jitsu, karate and groundwork. He is a state representative for many jujitsu, karate, judo and police instructors' organizations. He has done over 1000 shows and seminars.

Kenpo expert Steve Sanders was one of the co-founders of the Black Karate Federation (1970), and was one of the top U.S. competitors during the late 1960s and early 1970s. He was one of the best-known African American karate instructors and produced numerous West Coast champions.

# The 1970s

Three of karate toughest competitors during American Karate's "Blood and Guts" era, included, left to right: Roger Carpenter, Fred Wren and Bob Wall.

Cecil Peoples (right) was one of California's top karate competitors in the early 1970s. He was one of the first point fighters to enter full contact karate and later became a highly skilled referee for all types of full contact events.

Robin L. Rielly's book, **The History of American Karate**, started out as a Masters Thesis in Japanese Area Studies for Seaton Hall University and became the first book to examine this relatively new martial art in the United States. It was published in 1970 and covered all the various systems and styles coast to coast.

In the early 1970s when **Kung Fu** the T.V. show was on ABC, America experienced a "kung fu craze". Hundreds of schools across the country began teaching this Chinese art and dojos everywhere advertised kung fu. For a while kung fu seemed to be as popular as karate, but the craze was short lived and the art's popularity diminished by the late 1970s.

By the early 1970s many karate schools were teaching the use of various martial arts weapons. The most common weapons used were the sai, bo, kama, nunchaku and tonfa. Seen here is the sai (left) vs the bo.

One of the most spectacular demos at martial arts events was catching a razor sharp samurai sword with bare hands, an extremely dangerous move, as performed here by Tadashi Nakamura.

During the 1970s, Fumio Demura and a group of his black belts were hired by the Buena Park Japanese Deer Park to put on daily karate demonstrations. This was the first place in the United States to feature karate on a regular basis, and it led to a similar job for Demura at the Las Vegas Hilton Hotel. *Courtesy of F. Demura*

The 1970s

An audio-visual means of gaining expertise in the martial arts. By the 1970's promoters were dreaming up any way to get the public's money.

American karate champion and promoter, Joe Corley who teaches his own Joe Corley American Karate System, was a leading point karate fighter during the late 60's and early '70s. In 1974, he challenged Bill Wallace to a full contact world title fight, which he lost by a ninth round TKO. Corley was one of the biggest advocates of full contact karate and was the founder of the Battle of Atlanta Karate Championships, which began in 1970. Today, it is one of the largest martial arts events in the country.

By the early 1970s, Korean taekwondo was becoming widely practiced in the U.S. Parts of it's mass appeal was the spectacular aerial kicks that the art taught.

By the 1970s, martial arts was becoming a big business and companies such as this poster company were cashing in.

# An Illustrated History Of Martial Arts In America – 1900 to Present

If you couldn't be a 'real' champ at least you could pretend. These early 1970s ads claimed.

One of the earliest advertisements during the early 1970s capitalizing on the new kung fu craze.

1976: Shawnee Mission, Kansas
Jim Harrison with four of his PKA National Champions at his Bushidokan Mission Kansas Dojo. Left to right: Jeff Payne, Ray Patton, Jim Harrison, Payne and Steve Mackey.
***Courtesy of Jim Harrison***

Bow Tim Mark is a master instructor of the Chinese Martial Arts. Originally from Canton, China she moved to the United States in the early 1970s and founded the world famous Chinese Wushu Institute in Boston. She is especially noted for her Chinese sword skill, and for developing theatrical pieces that use authentic martial arts techniques to tell a story.

The 1970s

A group of top American Karate men seen at a team competition in the early 1970s. Standing (l-r): Arnold Urquidez, Ron Marchini, ?, Louis Delgado, ?, Malachi Lee, Ken Knudson, Jim Koncevic. Kneeling: Johnny Kuhl, Frank Ruiz, Ed Parker, Aaron Banks, Ernie Lieb, Jimmy Jones, Bill Wallace.

Chuck Merriman was one of America's top Kata competitors in the early 1970s. One of the most respected Goju-ryu instructors in the United States, Merriman went on to become a top coach and world class referee. He was the coach of the American karate team at the 5th WUKO World Championships in 1980, where Tokey Hill became the first American World Champion.

Malia Dacascos (Malia Bernal) was one of the leading female martial arts competitors in the early and mid 1970's. A Won Hop Kune Do stylist, during her prime Malia was among the best-known martial artist in the country.

# An Illustrated History Of Martial Arts In America – 1900 to Present

Joe Hess was a leading East Coast martial artist who was a top competitor during the early 1970s. A former student of Peter Urban, Hess became one of the first kickboxing champions in the United States. He has been heavily involved in law enforcement and is an expert Defensive Tactics instructor.

A photo in the early days of the ATA when master Lee was recruiting instructors to learn his system and then go to various parts of the U.S. to teach. From left to right: Gee Ho Lee, H.U. Lee, William Clark and Robert Allemier. Today Clark and Allemier remain the highest-ranking American members of the ATA. *Courtesy of the ATA*

A group of great American martial artist gather in Northern California in the early 1970's. Left to right: ?, Richard Kim, Herbert Lee, Chuck Norris, Richard Lee, Duke Moore, Kneeling left to right: Johnny Pereira, Leroy Rodriquez, ?.

The 1970s

Some of the greatest Karate experts of the 1970's. Back row (l-r) Ralph Castro, Ron Marchini, Alan Steen, Chuck Norris, Ed Parker, Skippers Mullins, Tony Tulliners (who lost in the internationals to Chuck Norris, Alan Steen and Mike Stone but finally took third) and Greg Baines who was knocked out by Joe Lewis in the first gloved kickboxing match). Front row (l-r) Arnold Urquidez and Mike Stone.

Chuck Loven (left) was a top rated karate champion in the early 1970s and student of Pat Burleson. After his retirement, he trained a number of champions, including Pat Worley, Larry Carnahan and Gary Hestilow Facing against Loven is Texas karate instructor, Duane Ethington, who became one of the earliest martial arts journalists in the United States.

Ron Chappel was one of Ed Parker's top black belts and was one of the founders of the Black Karate Federation, a leading group in the Southern California area during the 1970s and 1980s.

An Illustrated History Of Martial Arts In America – 1900 to Present

In 1975, Bob Wall wrote the first Who's Who in the Martial Arts. The book had 131 of the most prominent male & female martial artists plus a martial arts dictionary and listed the 5,023 martial arts schools then existing in the US.

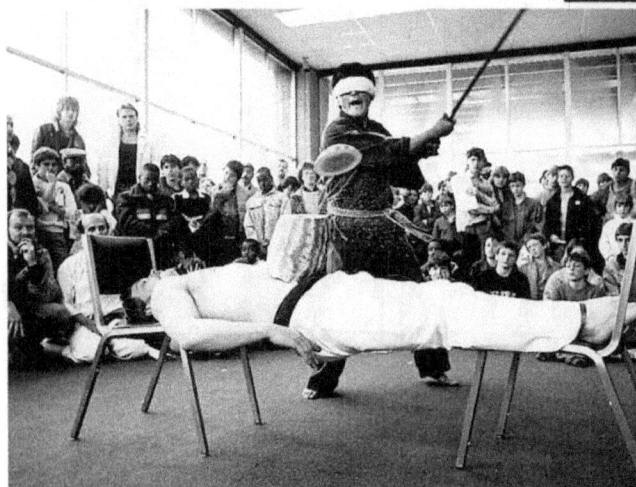

Tadashi Yamashita, one of the top weapons experts in the U.S., is seen here cutting a watermelon into 5 pieces while blindfolded.

Fred Wren is one of the greatest American karate champions. He was the number one fighter of the early 1970s and has been teaching karate since 1966. A former Texan, he now teaches in St. Louis. *Courtesy Official Karate*

The 1970s

Chinese-American Kung Fu champion Anthony Chan was one of the first martial artists in the United States to teach and promote modern Wushu. He was one of the founders of the San Francisco Wushu Team which became the leader in demonstrating and performing the art through the late 1970s and early 1980s.

Three leading American Karate Champions at the St. Louis Gateway Open Tournament in 1970. Left to right: Mike Stone, Phillip Koeppel, Chuck Norris. *Courtesy of P. Koeppel*

The Korean instructors were noted for their spectacular kicking demos at American karate tournaments in the early '70s. *Courtesy of George Anderson*

Some of the leading Korean instructors of the time at Henry Cho's All American Open Karate tournament in the early 1970s. *Courtesy of George Anderson*

An Illustrated History Of Martial Arts In America – 1900 to Present

Actor Steve McQueen (in dark t-shirt) is flanked by two of his martial arts instructors, Pat Johnson (left) and Chuck Norris. To the left of Pat is karate champion Howard Jackson. *Courtesy of P. Johnson*

Roger Carpenter, a student of George Pesare was the first New England karate champion in 1970. A top competitor in the late '60s and early '70s he fought a full contact grudge match (with no safety gear) against John Balee in 1973 and put him in the hospital. In 1965 he began teaching in Wichita, Kansas producing top students.

The Sherman Oaks Karate School, shown, was owned by Chuck Norris and Bob Wall (teaching). It was one of the first, large, modern karate dojos in Los Angeles and by 1970 had hundreds of students. *Courtesy of B. Wall*

The American team at the 1st World Karate Championships held in Tokyo on October 10, 1970. Left to right: Gene Takahashi, ?, James Yabe, John Gehlsen, Tony Tulleners, and George Sansano.

The 1970s

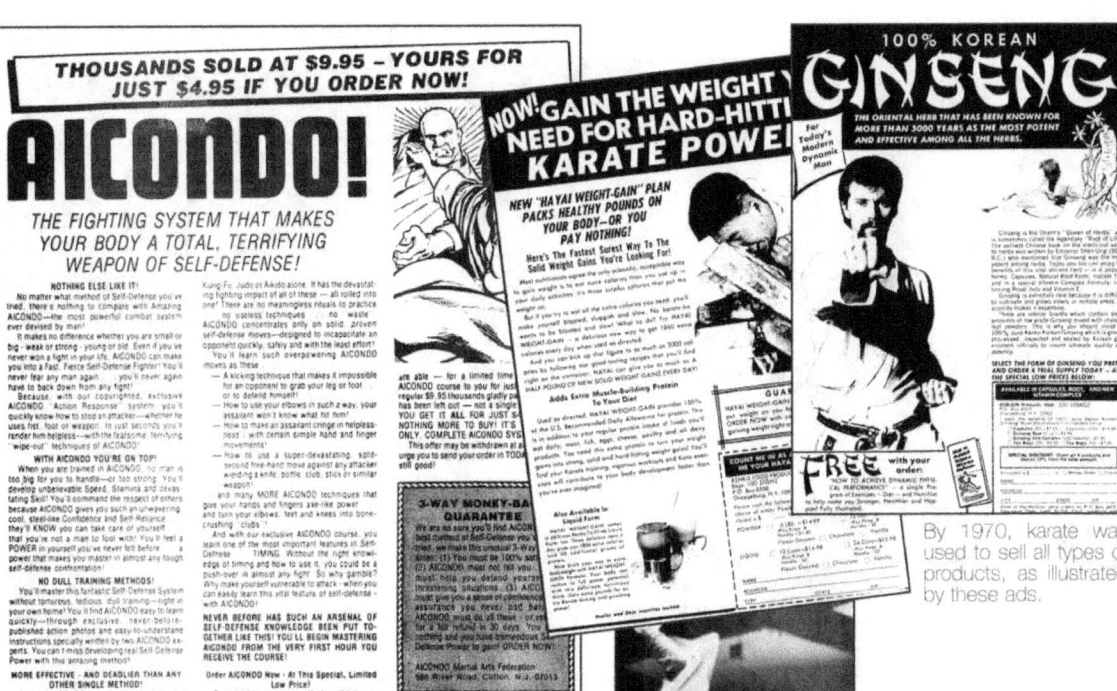

By 1970, karate was used to sell all types of products, as illustrated by these ads.

In the 1970s, dozens of 'made up' fighting systems, such as this one were being widely advertised and promoted to the general public.

New York-based Moses Powell was famous for his incredible one finger roll, demonstrated frequently at tournaments and expositions.

*Courtesy of Official Karate*

In 1970, promoter Lee Falker (3rd from right) gathered together sport karate's greatest fighters at the time and formed the first world professional karate team. The team defeated all comers during a prestigious tournament held at the Long Beach arena. Team members (l-r) included Bob Wall, Chuck Norris, Skipper Mullins, Mike Stone and Joe Lewis.

Bob Wall scoring a point and defeating Louie Delgado at the 1969 Internationals. The referee Pat Johnson didn't think it was a point until he saw the film. It was contact like this that led to the creation of the Penalty Point System in 1970, signifying the end of the Blood and Guts era. *Courtesy of Bob Wall*

An Illustrated History Of Martial Arts In America – 1900 to Present

Some early American karate champions, pose at Madison Square Gardens at a tournament held on March 7, 1971. Left to right: Tiger Kim, Henry Cho, (Promoter) Byong Yu, Joe Hayes, Mitchell Bobrow, Mike Warren.  *Courtesy of Mitchell Bobrow*

Ron Van Clief was one of the top karate competitors on the East Coast during the 1960s and 1970s and, at age 51, competed in the UFC in 1994. He has studied numerous martial arts with many well-known masters including Peter Urban, Eizo Shimabuku and Ting Leung. In 1971, he founded his own Chinese Goju style. He worked on numerous movies, including a series of Hong Kong films playing the role of the **"Black Dragon"**.
*Courtesy of Ron Van Clief*

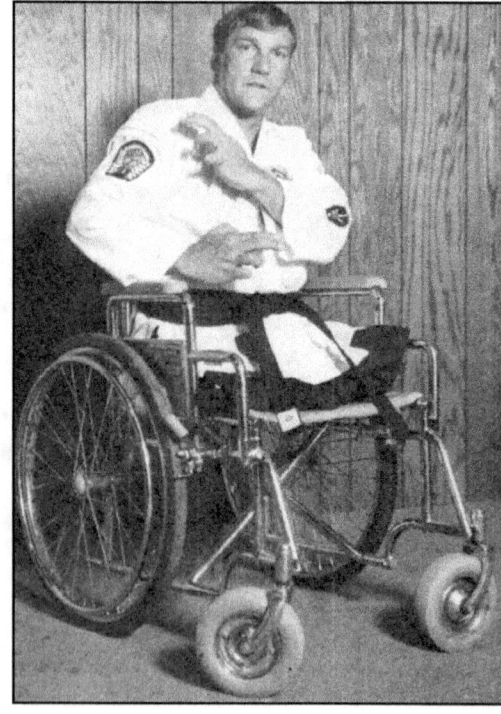

Ted Vollrath, of Harrisburg, PA, was the first person in the world to earn a black belt in karate while training from a wheel chair. Vollrath, who lost both his legs while serving in the United States Marine Corps in Korea, began training in 1967 and became a black belt in five years. He spent most of his time teaching the handicapped to look past their limitations. His incredible demonstrations at tournaments were a constant inspiration to everyone. In 1971, he founded Martial Arts for the Handicapable. He passed away on November 18, 2001.

## The 1970s

The 1971 film Billy Jack, starring Tom Laughlin (left) was the first American made movie to exploit the spectacular kicks of the martial arts. Bong Soo Hahn, a Hapkido expert, choreographed the spectacular fight sequences and became a martial arts celebrity. *Courtesy of Warner Brothers*

Jim Harrison (right) fought and defeated Vitor Moore in 1971 for the first U.S. Light Heavyweight Kickboxing Championship.

Pu Gill Gwon, a tae kwon do and judo expert, began his training as a teenager in his native Korea. In 1971, he came to the U.S and gained fame by performing spectacular breaking demos at various martial arts events. Besides his great teaching skills, he was also a well-known author with numerous books to his credit.

Some of the leading karate champions during the early 1970s are seen here at the East Coast vs Mid West Karate Championships in Chicago. Standing (l-r): Little John Davis, Bill Downs, Jimmy Jones, Joel B. Ward and Shorty Mills. Kneeling: Joe Hess, Jimmy Santiago, Owen Watson, Ron Van Clief and Preston Baker. *Courtesy of Mary Townsley*

An Illustrated History Of Martial Arts In America – 1900 to Present

The 1971 US judo team that won seven medals at the Pan American Judo Championships in Brazil (l-r): Paul Maruyama, Larry Fukuhara, Brian Yakata, Roy Sukimoto, Patrick Burris and Coach Ben Campbell.

In 1971 Bruce Lee appeared with James Franciscus in the **Longstreet** T.V. series. In the opening episode Lee not only got to show off his physical skill but also had an opportunity to explain some of the philosophical principals, which lay at the foundation of his art, Jeet Kune Do. The script was written by Lee's student, Sterling Silliphant.

Martial arts expert David Chow (right) began his study of kung fu in his native Shanghai. He moved to the United States as a teenager and got involved in judo, becoming California State Judo Champion at age 16. In 1972, he became the technical adviser and fight co-coordinator for the **Kung Fu** T.V. series. Here, is rehearsing a group of extras on the show.

The first book on this deadly Okinawan weapon, it was published in 1971 and authored by famous karate and weapons expert, Fumio Demura.

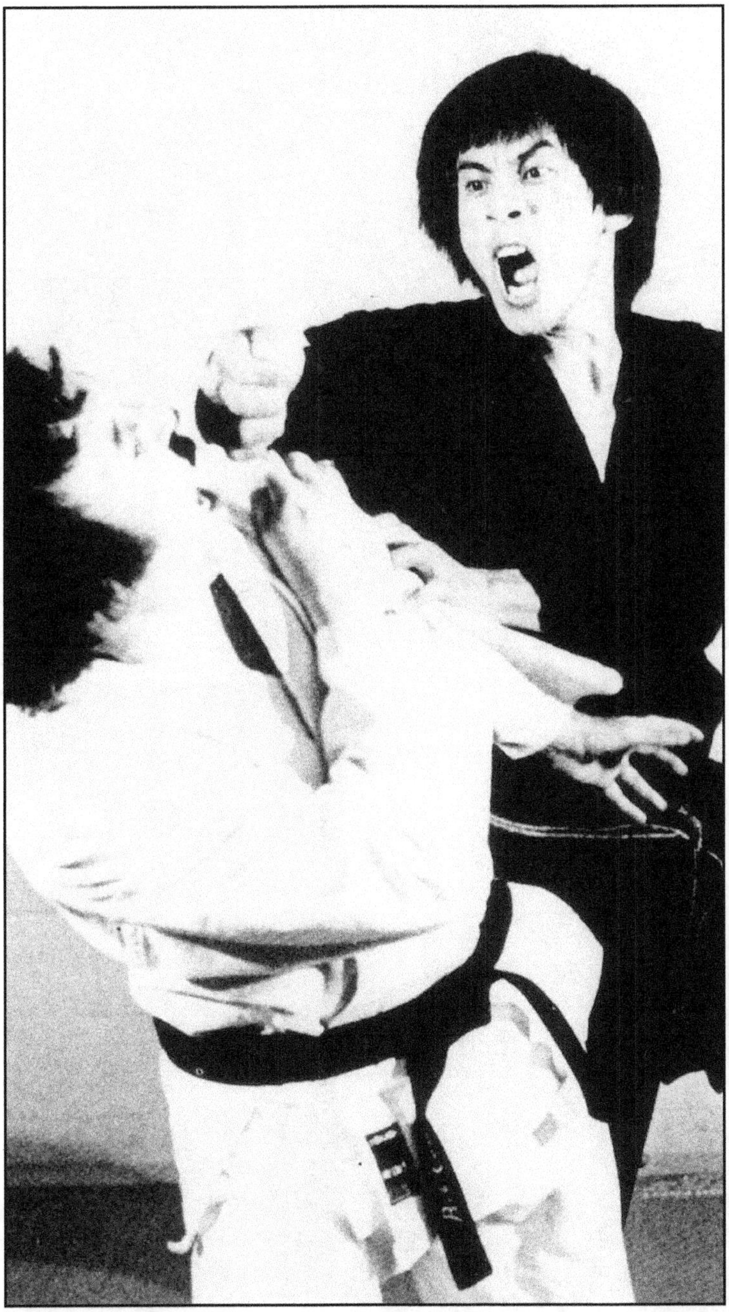

The 1970s

Pat Johnson was a top competitor in the 1960s and '70s, and captained the undefeated Chuck Norris team from 1969-73. Johnson, who was also a highly respected instructor, became one of the most successful fight co-coordinators in Hollywood, where he's worked on the **Karate Kid** movies, **The Ninja Turtle** films, **Force Five** and numerous other. *Courtesy of Pat Johnson*

Famous Korean-American karate champion, Byong Yu, is congratulated on his win at the 1971 All-American Open Karate Championships, by promoter Henry Cho. This tournament was one of the earliest and most prestigious in New York. *Courtesy of George Anderson*

Pete Rabino (in black) was one of the top fighters of the USKA and was one of its leading members. A student under Robert Trias he became one of the first chief instructors in 1971 and in 1974 was elected to the prestigious Trias international society. He teaches Shuri Ryu in Laguna Beach California. *Photo courtesy of Pete Rabino*

In 1972 Michael Staples was the first journalist to write about White Crane kung fu in a western periodical. A student of the arts since the mid-1950s, Staples learned White Crane in San Francisco from George Long. In 1974 he authored White Crane Kung Fu: Chinese Art of Self Defense. He later became a contributing editor to **Inside Kung Fu Magazine** and became one of the most knowledgeable westerners on the Chinese martial arts.

Hapkido expert Bong Soo Hahn was instrumental in popularizing his art when, in 1972, he choreographed the fight scenes for the hit movie **Billy Jack**. Moving from his native Korea to the United States in 1968, Hahn has become one of the best-known Korean martial arts instructors in the country. Over the years, he has worked in numerous films, including **The Kentucky Fried Movie**, **Force Five** and **The Trial of Billy Jack**. In 1974, he wrote the first book on Hapkido.

Darnell Garcia, who studied karate under Chuck Norris, was one of the top U.S. karate competitors in the early 1970s. In 1972, he won Ed Parker's prestigious Long Beach Internationals.

American karate pioneer Lou Casamassa studied both judo and karate in the Orient and opened his first dojo in 1964 in Pennsylvania. He gained a huge following and in 1973 he moved to Covina a Southern California suburb where he began his Red Dragon School, which now includes over 25 dojos. He was one of the first senseis to teach an eclectic American karate style.

The 1970s

Four great American karate fighters from Texas (l-r): Demetrius Havanis, Ed Daniels, Ronny Cox and Skipper Mullins. *Courtesy of Jerry Beasley*

Two of Okinawa's top karate masters, Hohan Soken (left) and Fusei Kisei (right) came to the U.S. in 1972, visiting with Glenn Premru (center).

Charles Bronson, on the set of the movie, **The Mechanic**, plays a hired killer who happens to be a karate expert. Standing to the left is karate master Tak Kubota and one of his top students, Hank Hamilton. Kubota was the fight choreographer on this 1972 film. *Courtesy of Tak Kubota*

Chuck Norris' black belt teams were undefeated from 1968 to 1974. Left to right: Bob Alegria, Pat Johnson, Clyde Mills, Chuck Norris, Dennis Young, Bob Wall, Victor Guerrero and Jerry Taylor.

Ken Knudson (left) shown attacking Walt Boone in 1972 was one of the top American fighters of the mid '60s and early '70s. Located in Chicago, he was one of the earliest business professionals in the martial arts with over 10 schools under him. *Courtesy of Mary Townsley.*

In 1972 Bruce Lee wrote, directed and starred in **Return of the Dragon**. The film featured karate champion Chuck Norris in a memorable fight against Lee. The movie was filmed in Rome's famous Coliseum. *Courtesy of Bob Wall.*

This book, published in a limited edition, is now a collector's item. It was released in 1973 but never sold in bookstores. The booklet is a manual of what Norris was teaching at the time, including forms.

*Courtesy of Beverly Hills Archives*

Producer Fred Weintraub (right) seen here with director Robert Clouse was one of the best-known Hollywood producers of martial arts themed movies. Among his credits are: **Enter the Dragon** (1973), **Black Belt Jones** (1974), **The Big Brawl** (1980), **Force Five** (1981), **The Master Ninja** (1984), **Gymkata** (1985) and **China O'Brian I** and **II**.

The 1970s

Curtis Wong (right) seen here with Ed Parker and Ginger Alden (Elvis Presley's ex-girlfriend), published the first American magazine devoted to the Chinese Martial Arts, **Inside Kung-Fu Magazine**. It was first published in 1973 and Wong went on to build a publishing empire with numerous other magazines and books devoted to the martial arts. *Courtesy of Inside Kung-Fu Magazine*

Sifu Kam Yuen, a leading kung fu instructor and expert in the Chinese healing arts, was asked in 1972 by Warner Brothers to be David Carradine's double in the ABC Kung Fu series. Eventually, he replaced David Chow as the fight coordinator of the series and became David Carradine's instructor. *Courtesy of Warner Brothers*

One of the most memorable and exciting karate matches in American karate history took place at the 1973 Long Beach Internationals, where John Natividad (right) defeated Benny Urquidez in a 23 point overtime match.

Canadian karate champion, Wally Slocki, attacks Flem Evans at the 1973 U.S.K.A. National Karate Championships. *Courtesy of Mary Townsley*

An Illustrated History Of Martial Arts In America – 1900 to Present

The first book published in the United States about Bruce Lee was Alex Ben Block's **The Legend of Bruce Lee**. The book was released in March, 1974, less then a year after Lee's death on July 20, 1973.

John P Painter is one of the pioneers of Chinese internal arts, which he teaches at his academy "The Gompa" in Arlington Texas. He opened the school in 1973, and was the first instructor to teach the Chinese arts in Texas.

Publisher Curtis Wong was one of David Carradine's stunt doubles on the TV show **Kung Fu**.

Football and movie star Fred Williamson became an avid martial artist after his starring role in **That Man Bolt** (1973). He's shown working out with his instructor Emil Farkas.

The 1970s

**Enter the Dragon**, released in 1973, made Bruce Lee a world-renowned celebrity and boosted the interest of martial arts in the U.S. enormously. Unfortunately, Lee passed away before the film's release by Warner Brothers. This photo was taken after the infamous bottle fight scene. *Courtesy of Bob Wall*

Barbara Niggel, a top kata competitor during the 1970s, was one of the first women in the United States to open a dojo. Teaching the Indonesian Martial Arts system of Poekoelan Tjimindie, she opened her school in 1973 in Lowellville, Ohio, while still a teenager.

Fred Absher (right) was a top American karate competitor during the 1960s and early 1970s. He captained the U.S. Taekwondo team at the first World Taekwondo Championships in Seoul, Korea, in 1973. In 1975 he was named chief instructor of the International Kojosho Karate Federation, which he oversees to this day.

Linda Denley, known as the "Texas Terror", was one of the best female karate fighters in the United States. She was ranked number one from 1973-1996 and won every major United States tournament numerous times. A Tang So Do stylist, Denley runs her own dojo in Houston.

# An Illustrated History Of Martial Arts In America – 1900 to Present

In the early 1970s, when kung fu became the new fad in martial arts, ads like these were quick to come along.

During the early 1970s, Howard Jackson (delivering a hook kick), became the number one non-contact karate fighter in the United States. He later became a world kickboxing champion and was one of the few martial artists to achieve fame in semi-contact karate, full contact karate, kickboxing and boxing. Howard passed away in 2006 at age 55.

Hong Kong produced the film, **Five Fingers of Death** which hit American movie houses in 1973. It was the first Chinese martial arts movie to be widely distributed in the U.S. and because of its success it made Hollywood more interested in distributing and making other films featuring martial arts action.

Canadian Wally Slocki began his competitive career in the mid-1960s and became one of the only Canadians to gain recognition in United States tournaments. He was Canadian Champion numerous times and won the prestigious U.S.K.A. Championships in Kata in 1973. He was one of the first instructors in North America to franchise schools.

The 1970s

Bruce Lee's grave site in Seattle, Washington at Lake view cemetery.

Huang Chien-Liang is one of the top Chinese martial arts master's in the US. Moving here in 1973, he has been instrumental in teaching and promoting the Chinese arts. He is the 64th generation Grand Master of Tien Shan Pai and has served as a head coach of the U.S. kuoshu team competing at the World Championships. He is the first inductee into the U.S. Koushu Hall of Fame in 2000.

On August 17, 1973, over 10,000 martial arts fans were treated to a display of skill by 35 of the world's greatest martial artists at **Black Belt Magazine**'s First Oriental Fighting Arts Expo. The event was dedicated to Bruce Lee.

**Inside Kung Fu Magazine** was started by Curtis Wong in 1973. The magazine has gone on to become one of the longest running regularly published martial arts magazines in the USA. The first issue had David Carradine (back) and David Chow on the cover.   *Courtesy of Curtis Wong.*

Shuri-ryu karate master Robert Bowles was the first person in the history of the United States Karate Association Grand Nationals to win the triple crown: 1st place in Kata, Kumite and Weapons. He won this incredible feat in 1973 and has held the title of USKA World Champion six times. A student under Robert Trias, Bowles is, today, one of the chief instructors of the Shuri-ryu system in the United States. *Courtesy of R. Bowles*

In the feature film **Cleopatra Jones**, Tamara Dobson uses her karate skills to fight off drug traffickers. This action thriller released by Warner Brothers in 1973, used Hapkido master Bong Soo Hahn as the fight coordinator. *Courtesy of Warner Brothers.*

Dan Anderson (left) seen here delivering a punch against Keith Vitali, was one of America's top rated semi-contact karate champions during the 1970s. The founder of "American Freestyle Karate", he won over seventy grand championship titles during his career. Anderson later became an expert in Arnis and today teaches in Gresham, Oregon.

Some of the top karate competitors in the United States at the Tournament of the Century held in 1973 in Chicago. L-r: Fred Wren, Bill Wallace, Glen Keeney, Owen Watson, Ron Van Clief and Little John Davis. Kneeling is Jimmy Jones. *Courtesy of M. Townsley.*

Byong Yu was a noted taekwondo instructor and a top competitor during the 1970s. His great kicking skills made him a favorite of the audience, and his breaking demos got standing ovations. He teaches today in Los Angeles. *Courtesy of Keith Yates*

## The 1970s

In 1973, former football star turned actor, Fred Williamson starred in the action film **That Man Bolt**. Williamson plays Jefferson Bolt, an international courier, who is a martial arts expert and has to transport one million dollars from Hong Kong to Mexico City. The film has plenty of martial arts action performed by Williamson and numerous named martial artists who perform stunt work on the movie. *Courtesy of Universal Pictures*

Ron Van Clief (right) was one of the first karate champions to begin doing films in Hong Kong. He began a series of Black Dragon Films in 1973 and is seen here in **The Death of Bruce Lee**. *Courtesy Ron Van Clief*

Some of America's top traditional karate Champions and senseis line up at the first Pan American Karate Championships in 1973. Their coach was world famous Shotokan Sensei Hidetaka Nishiyama (in suit). From left to right: C. Avilar, G. Evans, Ed Geeter, J. Fields, D. Vaughn, H. Nishiyama, Frank Smith, Brurrel, Richard Kim and T. Okazaki. *Courtesy of James Fields*

Two leading karate champions of the mid 1970s were Roy Kurban (left) and Darnell Garcia. Here Kurban scores a point on Garcia at the Western Grand Nationals in 1974 in Oakland, California.
*Courtesy of Roy Kurban*

1976: Inglewood, CA
Heavyweight Champion Ken Norton (left), and Leo Fong at Bill Slayton's 108th Street Broadway Gym. This photograph was taken before Ken Norton's second match against Muhammad Ali.
*Courtesy of Leo Fong*

Joe Lewis (left) stalks Steve Sanders at the 1974 PAWAK Championships. Lewis won the grand title by defeating Sanders.

Jeff Smith was one of the leading semi-contact karate champions in the U.S. during the early 1970s. In 1974, he became full contact karate's first world professional light-heavy weight champion, and became one of the few karate competitors to become a full contact champion as well. A student of Jhoon Rhee, Smith became a top instructor and coach after he quit competition. He is seen here (left) fighting European karate champion Dominic Valera.

# The 1970s

In the early 1970s, the Kung Fu craze in America began. The first book in English to explore the history and philosophy of Kung Fu came out in 1974.

Left to right: Bill Wallace, Jeff Smith and Joe Lewis became the world's first professional full contact karate champions on Sept. 14, 1974. Each won a world championship title: Wallace (middleweight), Smith (light-heavyweight) and Lewis (heavyweight). *Courtesy of Jerry Beasley*

Korean martial arts master In Hyuk Suh is the founder of Kuk Sool Won a Korean fighting system that today has over one million followers. Born in Korea, Suh moved to the United States in 1974 and a year later formed the World Kuk Sool Association which today has its headquarters in Houston, Texas.

In 1974, American Karate champion Mike Stone conceived the Golden Fist Awards, which honored leading martial arts pioneers and champions. Here, Howard Jackson (left) and Darnell Garcia receive their Golden Fist Awards.

An Illustrated History Of Martial Arts In America – 1900 to Present

American karate pioneer and promoter Mike Anderson is perhaps best known as one of the originators of full-contact karate. In 1974, he co-produced the first World Professional Karate Championship and became the leading advocate of professional karate when he founded Professional Karate Magazine in 1972. A student of Allen Steen and a former leading competitor, his Top 10 Nationals, was one of the major karate tournaments of the 1970s.

"Monster Man" Eddy (left) and Bob Alegria fight it out at the 1974 Long Beach Internationals. Referee is Jerry Piddington with Steve Armstrong judging on the side.

This was the first book in English dealing with Martial Arts in the Cinema. It was published in 1974.

By the time the first **National Collegiate Judo Handbook** was published in 1974, close to 300 colleges and universities had a judo program.

In 1974, this series of pocket books appeared featuring Jason Striker, an expert in karate, kung fu and aikido. The 6 books in the series were published to cash in on the kung fu/karate craze that was sweeping America.

Ki Yun Yi, one of the leading Korean martial arts instructors in the United States, he came here in 1974 to teach Tang Soo Do and decided to stay. He opened a dojo in 1975 in Woodbury, New Jersey. In 1984, he founded the International Martial Arts Association, whose aim is to retain the traditionalism paramount to the true spirit of Tang Soo Do.

Famous martial arts historian Richard Kim authored **The Weaponless Warrior** in 1974. It was the first book in English exploring the history of Okinawan karate.

The 1970s

This tournament, held in 1974 was the first to be allowed to take place in Beverly Hills. Although not as large as many major events, the tournament had the distinction of drawing more major Hollywood stars as spectators than any other event past or present. It gave karate great exposure to people in the entertainment field, especially at a time when the martial arts movie genre was just developing.

Rusty Kanakogi was a pioneer of sport judo for women. In 1961, she entered an all male judo tournaments and won, and from then on she worked incessantly to get the sport to allow women to compete. By 1974 the AAU consented and competition in judo for women began. She is today considered one of the most respected instructors and administrators in judo.
*Courtesy R. Kanakogi*

Joe Lewis receives the World Heavyweight Full Contact Championship trophy from Telly Savalas (Kojak) at the L.A. sports arena on Sept. 14, 1974. Promoter Mike Anderson announcing.
*Courtesy of Mike Anderson*

Steve Armstrong, Isshin Ryu stylist, is seen refereeing two top fighters.

Phil Koeppel, on the extreme left, is seen along with many of the mid-west's top masters.

Fumio Toyoda was one of the leaders of Aikido in America. Settling in Chicago in 1974, he eventually founded the Aikido Association of America, and worked hard to propagate true Aikido by certifying instructors.

141

An Illustrated History Of Martial Arts In America – 1900 to Present

Hapkido, which was introduced to the United States in 1964, did not become popular until its spectacular kicks were ably demonstrated in the **Billy Jack** movies of the early 1970s. Hapkido expert, Bong Soo Hahn, was responsible for choreographing the spectacular fights. Master Hahn is seen here showing off his kicking skill in the 1974 film **The Trial of Billy Jack**.

James Bond, 007, (Roger Moore) receives a savage kick from one of the many martial arts experts he is pitted against in **The Man With a Golden Gun**, a United Artists release (1974). *Courtesy of United Artists*

**The Black Samurai** was a pulp fiction series of books written in the 1970s. Its hero is Robert Sand, a G.I. on leave in Japan during the Vietnam War who becomes a disciple of an ancient Japanese trainer of warriors. The series was written by Marc Olden who was a black belt in karate and aikido.

The first book on Hapkido was published in 1974, and authored by Master Bong Soo Han of **Billy Jack** fame.

The 1970s

Parker Shelton scores with his trademark flying back fist.

On September 21, 1975, Gordon Franks (right) defeated Mexico's Ramiro Guzman to become contact karate's first super lightweight world champion. Referee is Jim Harrison.

**Bruce Lee memorial watch and alarm clock.**
Now you can own this digital watch or alarm clock honoring the late Bruce Lee for only $29.95, plus $1.00 pstg. & hndlg. Both timepieces guaranteed for a full 2 years. Also order your full color Bruce Lee poster for only $3.00. Order yours today!

Star-timers, 7168 Melrose Av. Dept.1431 L.A., Ca 90046

☐ I enclose $_____ for _____watch(es), _____ alarm clock(s).
☐ I enclose $_____ for ____ posters.
Sorry, no C.O.D.'s.
Name: _____
Address: _____
City/State/Zip: _____
California residents add sales tax

Not too long after Bruce Lee's death in 1973, everything with Lee's name on it was being sold nationwide, like this Bruce Lee "Memorial watch" honoring the "Little Dragon".

Bradley Steiner was one of the first American martial artists to devote his teaching to self-defense on the street. He founded the American Combato System in 1975 and has written numerous books on practical street defense. An expert in military hand-to-hand combat, Bradley started the International Combat Martial Arts Federation in the early 1980s.

An Illustrated History Of Martial Arts In America – 1900 to Present

In the 1970s, Shag Okada was one of America's top judo coaches. He was the coach of the 1975 Pan American judo team, which brought home 9 medals. Okada resides and teaches in Southern California.

In 1976, he was inducted as judo instructor of the year into the Black Belt Hall of Fame.

On January 4, 1975, New York instructor Fred Hamilton promoted the first bare-knuckle full contact professional tournament in the United States.

Hamilton, who ran a dojo in Harlem, was noted for using karate as a vehicle to reach people in trouble.

He passed away in 1986.

The movie **Killer Elite** (1975) was one of the first big American pictures to feature Ninjas. The movie, directed by Sam Peckinpah and starring Jimmy Caan, featured a number of well-known martial artists from Hollywood who were hired to add realism to the movie. Here, Jimmy Caan is shown with fight coordinator Emil Farkas, dressed as a ninja, rehearsing a fight scene. *Courtesy of Beverly Hills Archives*

# The 1970s

In the mid 1970s, American karate instructor Ted Kresge compiled an unpublished **Encyclopedia Of The Martial Arts**. This amazing work consisted of 40 chapters, 5000 pictures, 1100 pages and over 200,000 words and weighed 9 pounds.

The first book by Chuck Norris, revealing the techniques that made Norris the most popular American karate champion of the time. Published in 1975.

Ross Scott, a former U.S.K.A. karate competitor, became a P.K.A. world heavy weight karate champion after Joe Lewis's retirement. In 1975, he won a decision against Lewis.

On October 4th and 5th, 1975, the Third World Karate-do Championships took place in Long Beach, California. This WUKO sponsored tournament was the largest traditional karate tournament in the world, with over 70 countries participating.

A Canadian wildlife authority and karate instructor, C.W. Nicol, wrote **Moving Zen** in 1975. In the book, Nicol describes the difficulties a Caucasian karate student faces while training in Japan. The book was the first of its type in which great insight is given to the "real traditional" training that goes on in Japan, by someone who spent many years training there.

## An Illustrated History Of Martial Arts In America – 1900 to Present

**RULED UNLAWFUL**—Nunchaku sticks, ancient karate weapons, are examined by Officers Robert Villarino, left, and James Johnson. Nunchaku has been classified as a blackjack, illegal to possess.

By the mid-1970s, martial arts weapons became very controversial and laws were passed making it illegal to carry them or have them in a car.

On October 1, 1975, American karate champion Jeff Smith defeated Kariem Allah in a full-contact match. The fight, which played on closed circuit television as part of the Ali-Frazier "Thriller In Manila" was watched by 50 million viewers worldwide. Smith won a split decision in the 11-round bout. *Courtesy Jeff Smith.*

1975 - Tiger's Revenge
Leo Fong - one the early Karate pioneers who produced, starred and directed martial arts movies, in the 70's.
***Courtesy of Leo Fong***

The 1970s

By the mid 1970s, Americans were buying martial arts weapons of all types. This telescopic baton was a big seller.

American Kenpo instructor, Nick Cerio, became probably the best-known instructor in the Rhode Island area after opening a dojo in the mid-1960s. Much respected, he became highly visible throughout the United States after 1974, when he founded his own new system, Nick Cerio Kenpo.

While many Americans were drawn to the martial arts to learn to fight, many others liked the Oriental traditions and philosophy that went with the training.

Lilly Rodriquez (left) was the first female American kickboxing champion in the mid-1970s. A former non-contact karate champion, she followed her brother, Benny Urquidez, into the full contact arena. In the mid-'70s, Lily also became the first female California boxing champ. She passed away in 2007.
*Courtesy of Benny Urquidez*

An Illustrated History Of Martial Arts In America – 1900 to Present

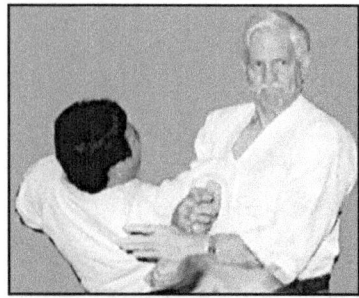

George Anderson was one of the leading martial arts administrators in the U.S. A former president of AAU, he was also a president of the Pan American Karate Union. Anderson who was a top administrator of WUKO was a referee at the 1975 WUKO World Championships and was a member of the prestigious Trias international society. Anderson began his martial arts training in 1950 and holds black belts in various fighting arts.

A group photo taken in 1975 at a California Vs Chicago tournament. On the left is Tino Tulesiega, ?, Benny Urquidez, Arnold Urquidez, Blinky Rodriguez, ?.
*Courtesy of Mary Townsley*

Sydney Pollack, one of Hollywood's most respected directors, filmed **The Yakuza** in 1975. The picture filmed in Japan, and starred Robert Mitchum and Ken Takura (shown here battling a Yakuza member). The film featured some of the most exciting samurai sword fighting ever filmed for an American movie and included some of Japan's leading sword masters playing Yakuza members. *Courtesy of Warner Brothers*

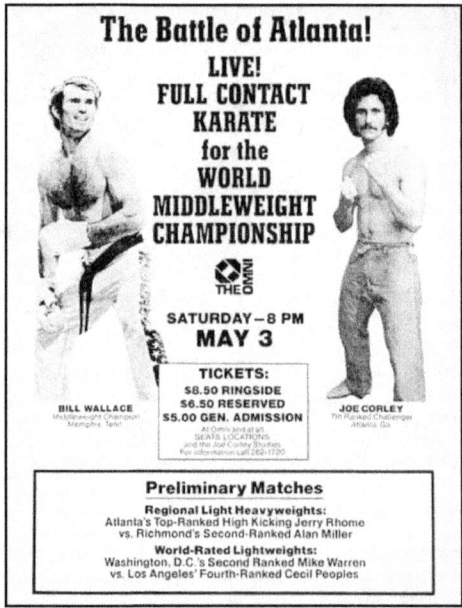

This was one of the most awaited fights in American karate history. On May 3, 1975, over 10,000 spectators filled the Omni Arena to see Wallace retain his crown with a 9th round TKO.
*Courtesy of Joe Corley.*

Julius Thiery (left), Steve Armstrong (center), and Allen Steen at a USKA Banquet in 1975.
*Courtesy of Mary Townsley*

The 1970s

American judo champion, Allen Coage, (shown holding down his opponent) was a bronze medalist at the 1976 Montreal Olympics in the heavy weight division. He was also a winner of two gold medals at the Pan American Games. In 1977 he became a pro wrestler.

Athlete of The Year, Muhammad Ali, stands next to Jhoon Rhee who was honored as the Martial Arts Man of the Century at the Touchdown club's Bi-centennial Sports Tribute in Washington, D.C., in 1976.

Pat Worley (left), seen here defeating Mike Warren at the 1970 Washington D.C. Nationals, was one of the leading United States karate competitors during the 1970s. He is one of the original founders of the Diamond National Karate Championships.

# An Illustrated History Of Martial Arts In America – 1900 to Present

One of America's leading martial arts journalists, John Corcoran was one of the first legitimate black belts to become an editor of Black Belt Magazine and Karate Illustrated. A protégé of Joe Lewis, Corcoran went on to author numerous books, and is the co-author of the Martial Arts Encyclopedia, one of the most comprehensive books ever written on the Martial Arts.

Kevin Parsons, a member of the U.S.K.A., was a police self defense authority and was the law enforcement liaison director for the United States Karate Association. He has authored numerous books and articles dealing with police self-defense and the use of various police weapons by law enforcement agencies.

Jerry Thomson was one of the most recognized traditional karate referees in the United States during the 1970s. In 1975, he became the AAU Officials Certification chairman for the United States and in 1977 became AAU Karate Sports chairman. He was the chief referee at the 4th WUKO World Championships in Tokyo in 1977.

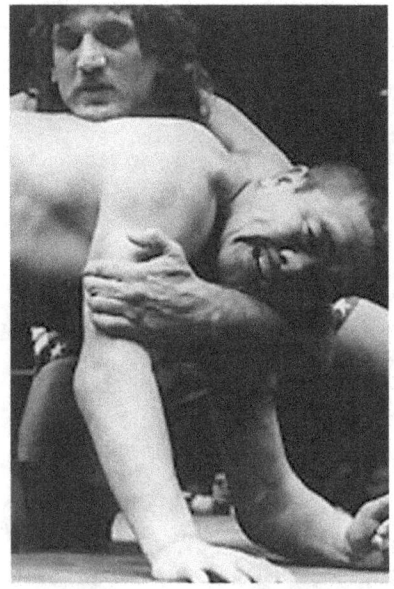

Former world shootfighting champion Bart Vale, began his training with Al Tracy's Kenpo Karate Organization. After competing as kickboxer, Vale trained in grappling and freestyle fighting under Masami Soranaka & Yoshiaki Fujiwara (pictured above).

By the mid-1970s, full contact karate was beginning to become accepted and audiences were expecting promoters to put on full contact bouts even at non-contact tournaments.

## The 1970s

Rod Sacharnosky, an instructor in numerous internal martial arts systems, gained fame during the 1970s with his demonstrations of combat ki, in which he and his students would take full power kicks and strikes to vital areas of the body, including the groin, without injury. His amazing demonstrations were featured on many of the major T.V. talk shows, including the **Johnny Carson Show**. He is seen here demonstrating a throw.

Monsterman Everett Eddy (left) seen here with promoter Aaron Banks was one America's top competitor during the 1970s.

In the 1970s famous karate sensei, Tak Kubota (seen here), developed a simple weapon called the Kubotan. This small plastic rod, which is a key-holder, could be used to strike or jab an attacker. The weapon became fairly popular especially with women.

The beauty and grace of the Chinese martial arts was a big reason many Americans got involved in it. Kung fu, unlike karate, attracted people who weren't just looking for self-defense skills.

Three of America's top female karate competitors during the 1970s included, from left to right: Maryanne Corcoran, Mike Rowe and Pauline Short (who was one of the first karate instructors to open a dojo exclusively for women in 1965).

Due to the interest in kung fu during the 1970s, books such as this one by Ohara Publications, were selling widely within the martial arts community.

A perfect flying sidekick performed by Mike Stone, one of the American legendary Karate champions.

By the 1970s, competitors at karate tournaments were wearing a variety of uniforms. At many open tournaments the traditional white gi was often rarely seen.

Gary Dill, one of the leading Jeet Kune Do instructors in the U.S., began training with James Lee at the Oakland dojo in 1971 and has continued to teach ever since. He is the head of Self Defense Systems, International Combat Martial Arts Federation and is dedicated to the training of combat related martial arts.

The 1970s

**Women Get Tough**

By HELENE FINE

Twenty soft, feminine women are discovering their power! In an age where crimes of violence are rising 10 times as fast as our population, and rapes are up 115 per cent, a woman needs all the protection she can get.

These feminists, ranging from 12 to 77 years of age, spend one hour, twice a week learning how to synchronize their body movements, act out their aggressive instincts and most important, discover vital areas of attack.

They are studying Kenpo Karate, a sport discovered in India hundreds of years ago by a Buddhist Monk and practiced today as a means of meditation and self defense. Only the fittest females will survive, so the training is tough.

Their husky bearded trainer is Tom Kelley, an ex-Marine with eight years of teaching experience under his black belt.

He dresses in a two-piece black canvas Karate uniform called a Gi, with large leather weights tied to each ankle and wrist for muscle conditioning.

The philosophy of peace and love is dismissed when the women enter the studio. "You approach your opponent and attack him as an enemy." Kelley insists, "and you're out to get him the quickest way possible."

"You aim for a quick strike in the temples with a closed fist," he said and quickly adds, "You want to get to your opponent before he gouges one of your eyes out." There is no time for procrastination in this art. "Nothing works like a good kick in the groin. It's immediate with no time lapse."

Karate students learn to totally depend on their own body strength. "You develop an ability to react to any situation which gives you a fantastic taste of inner security and self confidence.

"You build up a different kind of living pattern," Kelley said. "You learn to admire and respect more of your immediate environment, move about freely with a kind of inner security that makes you feel safe any place in the world."

How does a fragile woman respond to this kind of aggressive, going in for the kill kind of approach? Kelley admits to her squeamishness. "Girls don't like getting bruised or hit. They like to brag about taking Karate classes but it rubs against their passive non-violent nuiature."

But one of his female students was able to hit an attacker in the temple area and avoided being raped.

How many lessons before you can take on some big, burly attacker: A one-hour lesson twice weekly for 6 months to one year will prepare you for any opponent.

Student uses kick against instructor Tom Kelley

With crime on the increase during the 1970s, newspaper articles like these appeared all over the country, talking about the need for self-defense classes for women.

Jay T. Will was one of America's leading Kenpo karate instructors, and during the 1970s, was a top tournament competitor. When full contact karate began, Will became one of the most sought after referees of the new sport and was honored as PKA referee of the year for 1982 and 1983. He passed away in 1995.

Even before the Ninja craze of the 1980s, advertisements like this were appearing in comic books and magazines.

In the mid 1970's with traditional karate still the dominant style in America printing companies promoted these types of posters to the tens of thousands of Shotokan practitioners.

In the 1970s, Kung Fu became more popular with practitioners of all ages.

Combat Karate expert, Richie Barathy, was one of the greatest breakers in the U.S. During the 1970s, he was very visible because of his exhibitions at tournaments.

Due to the non-sportive aspect of Aikido, relatively few Americans embraced the art, although by the mid-1970s, it had a small but dedicated following. After Steven Seagal used Aikido in his film, **Above The Law**, the art did get a lot more popular.

Robert "Sugar" Crosson, a student of Moses Powell, was one of the greatest martial arts showmen in America. His martial arts and gymnastic skills were very visible during the 1970s with Aaron Bank's Oriental World of Self Defense, and his incredible speed became legendary. He teaches his own eclectic style of Sugar-Ryu Ju Jitsu in New York.

For the millions of people interested in Kung Fu, Karate or Self Defense . . . here is the answer! John Natividad's eight deadly courses of International Self Defense can be learned in your own home in only 30 minutes a day.

The very first hour after you receive the 8 courses you will be on your way to develop powerful self DEFENSE KNOW HOW that will help you in any tough situation.

It doesn't matter how small or large you are; whether you are weak or strong; young or old . . . this fantastic method of self defense could SAVE YOUR LIFE or a loved one.

One of the earliest karate champions to go on national TV to sell a self-defense course was John Natividad, who was promoting his course in the 1970s. Natividad, a student of Chuck Norris, was one of the '70s greatest competitors.

## The 1970s

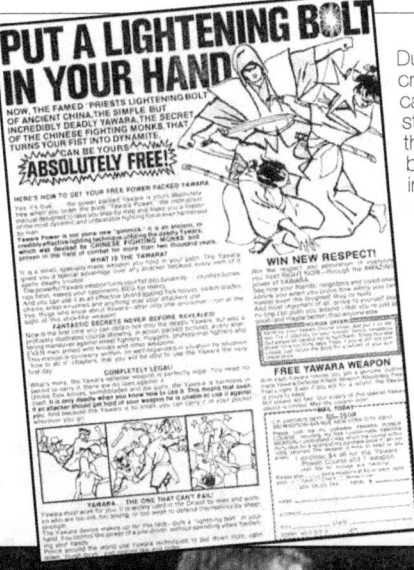

Due to increase in crime, the easy to carry yawara stick, invented in the 1940s, again became popular in the 1970s.

One of the most dangerous demonstrations at karate tournaments during the 1970s was the use of the nunchaku to obliterate objects that were held in someone's mouth (above). These types of demos made the nunchaku the most widely practiced martial arts weapons at the time.

Earnest Hart jr. (right) became the world welterweight kickboxing champion in 1977. He retired from competition in 1987 and currently teaches in the St. Louis area.

An Illustrated History Of Martial Arts In America – 1900 to Present

Ads like this during the 1970s made Tracy's the biggest karate franchise in the U.S. at that time.

**Budo**, released in 1979, was the first theatrical documentary featuring some of Japan's greatest martial artists.

Americans seldom saw many of the martial arts featured in this film.

*Courtesy of Crown International*

During the 1970s Kung fu books like these became very popular.

World Kata Champion, George Chung, became famous during the late 1970s for combining taekwondo techniques with gymnastics. His creative katas were consistent crowd pleasers. His famous 'Silver Bullet' was a kata done to the music of the Lone Ranger and everyone doing musical kata tried to top it. Next to George is female kata champion, Cynthia Rothrock.

James Benko, seen here demonstrating a twisting kick, began his martial arts training in 1959 and is, today, one of the leading American experts in Taekwondo, Hapkido and Shim Soo Do (Way of the Korean Sword). A former Green Beret, Benko founded the International Taekwondo Association, which has schools all over the world. Benko has authored numerous books on the Korean martial arts, and is publisher and editor of a number of Korean publications, including the Tae Kwon Do Journal.

# The 1970s

Former middleweight karate champion, Jim Kelly, got his start in the film industry when he appeared in a movie called **Melinda** in 1972. A year later, he co-starred in **Enter The Dragon**, which bought him "star status." He went on to star in **Black Belt Jones** (1974) and **The Black Samurai** (1976) and co-starred in **Three the Hard Way** (1974). He is seen here defeating Peter Marshal in a scene from **Enter the Dragon**. *Courtesy of Warner Brothers*

In the late 1970s, Daniel Duby was the first Savate instructor to begin teaching this French martial art in the U.S.

John Worley (left) and Pat Worley (right) were brothers who were among the leading karate champions in the United States during the 1970s. They later went on to open a chain of karate schools in the Minneapolis area. Seen here are some of their students – next to John is Gordon Franks, Gary Hestilow and Floyd Jackson.

Taekwondo expert, Ernie Reyes, is one of the best-known and highly respected martial artists in the U.S. During the 1970s, Reyes was a top tournament champion, but his biggest fame came from developing the world famous West Coast Demo Team, who traveled the United States putting on spectacular martial arts demonstrations. Reyes' son, Ernie, became the youngest black belt to compete and win against adults in kata. *Courtesy Ernie Reyes.*

An Illustrated History Of Martial Arts In America – 1900 to Present

A flyer for the Tennessee Karate Institute during the early to mid-'70s.

By the mid-1970s, hundreds of karate tournaments were being held all over the country. In any major American city often two or three tournaments were promoted almost every month. Most of these events were held in high school gyms or rented theatres where, often 10 to 15 rings were going simultaneously.

John Longstreet, a student of John Worley, was one of America's top karate champions from 1979 to 1983. He later turned to full-contact karate. Longstreet won the International Sport Karate Association (ISKA) World Middleweight Championship in September 1986 when he knocked out John Moncayo.
*Courtesy of Jerry Beasley*

In the early- and mid-1970s, it was not karate but kung fu that was supposed to make you a deadly oriental fighting master. And for only $2.95.

The 1970s

![Group photo of Shotokan instructors and karate campers]

Karate camps became prevalent in the United States after the mid-1970s, especially with the larger traditional karate organizations. Here, a number of America's top Shotokan instructors line up with a group of karate campers. Front line (l-r): J. Fields, S. Koyama, T. Mikami, T. Okazaki, Y. Yaguchi, S. Takashina, R. Dalke. *Courtesy of Ray Dalke*

Larry Carnahan (executing a beautiful side kick to Jeff Payne), was among the top ten lightweight kickboxers in the U.S. in the late 1970s. Before that, he was a leading semi-contact fighter and, in 1983, he became one of the founders of NASKA (North American Sport Karate Association). In 1984, he became its president. Carnahan is also one of the principles behind the Diamond Nationals, one of the top tournaments in the United States.

California's Steve Fisher, receiving a kick from Keith Vitali, was one of the top ranked fighter and kata competitors in the U.S. during the late '70s.

# An Illustrated History Of Martial Arts In America – 1900 to Present

Some of American karate's great senseis gather in the late 1970s. Left to right: Parker Shelton, Glen Keeney, Phillip Koeppel and James McLain.  *Courtesy of Phil Koeppel.*

By the end of the 1970s, more and more kids were practicing martial arts, and many were drawn to taekwondo because of the flashy kicks.

By the late 1970 safety equipment of all types were being used. Some tournaments encouraged the use of safety helmets, but few made them mandatory.

Young Steven Seagal moved to Japan to study aikido and became one of the best American aikido experts before returning to America in the 1970s.

The 1970s

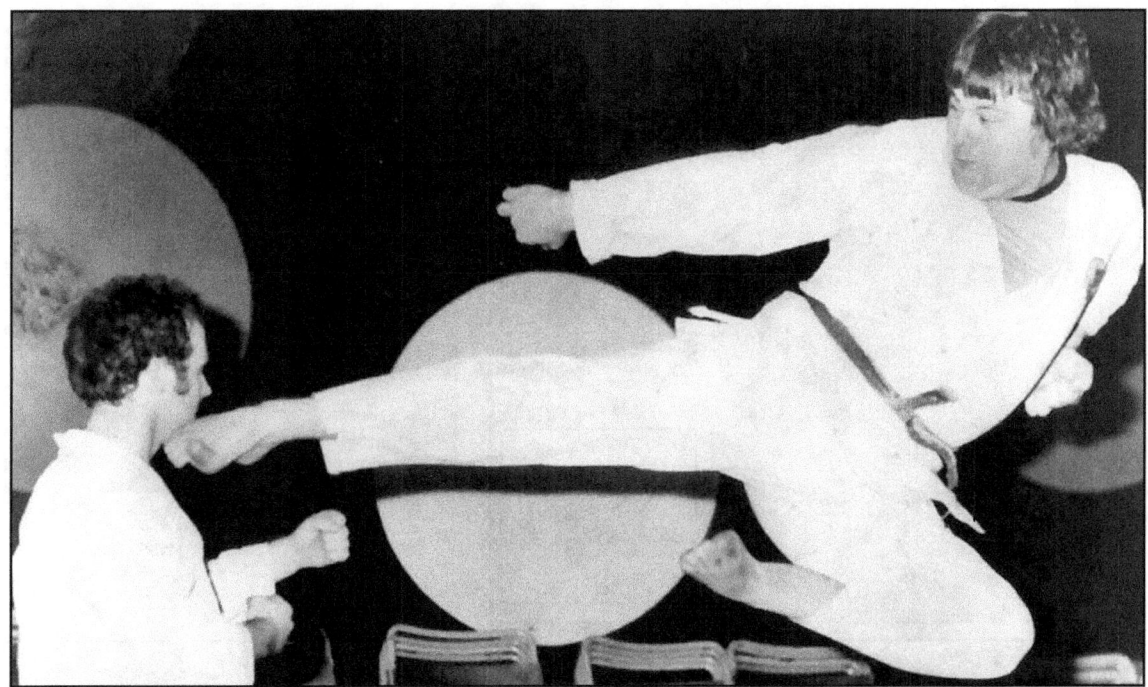

Don Warrener, a Canadian Goju-ryu karate instructor, was one of the first to have multiple schools in North America during the 1970s. A highly visible martial artist and student of Richard Kim, he moved to Los Angeles in the '90s, and founded his own multi-functional company, Rising Sun Productions.

Anthony Goh, one of America's most respected Chinese martial arts instructors, is noted for his organizational skills. As president of the USA Wushu Kung Fu Federation, he has been instrumental in spreading the Chinese arts in the U.S. and worldwide. He resides on the East Coast, where he has been teaching since 1979.

Howard Hanson was one of the pioneers of full contact karate when he founded the World Karate Association (WKA) in 1976, which became one of the biggest sanctioning bodies for the new sport.

Published in 1977, this was the first 'question and answer' book on the martial arts. With over 500 questions and answers, this book was instrumental in getting more reference books on the martial arts to be published in the U.S.

An Illustrated History Of Martial Arts In America – 1900 to Present

Chuck Norris plays a trucker with plenty of martial arts skills in the movie **Breaker, Breaker**. Released in 1977, it was his first starring role.

Bill Wallace (left) embraces Blinky Rodriguez after a tough full contact karate match in 1977 in Las Vegas. Wallace retained his middleweight world title by winning a decision. CBS TV filmed the P.K.A. sanctioned event, the first time full contact karate was broadcast live on network television. *Courtesy of Blinky Rodriguez*

**The Amazing Spiderman** T.V. show, which premiered on April 19, 1977, on CBS, featured plenty of martial arts action. Here, fight coordinator Emil Farkas faces off against Spiderman in one of the show's numerous action sequences.

The 1970s

The great Demetrius "Greek" Havanas - fabled Texas kickboxer, with a record of 43 wins and 2 losses, fought from 1970 to 1981 where he was tragically killed in a plane crash.

Famous Hapkido master, Bong Soo Hahn, played the role of the evil Mr. Hahn in the comedy spoof **Kentucky Fried Movie** (1977). Evan Kim parodies Bruce Lee in the longest segment of the film, which is based on **Enter the Dragon**.

Roger Moore playing James Bond in **The Spy Who Loved Me**, (1977), delivers a disabling side kick to his antagonist, Milton Reed, during a deadly fight on a rooftop in Cairo. *Courtesy of United Artists*

An Illustrated History Of Martial Arts In America – 1900 to Present

The ATA moved it's headquarters to Little Rock, Arkansas, in 1977, where they began to host a national tournament which today has become the ATA World Championships. The tournament draws over 25,000 competitors and spectators, and is the biggest yearly event in the city today. *Courtesy of the ATA*

Bruce Lee and Kareem Abdul-Jabbar put on a memorable fight in the film **Game of Death**, which was released in 1978, five years after Lee's death.

In 1978, the first issue of **Samurai Magazine** was published. This was the first U.S. magazine to focus on traditional karate. On the cover is Hidetaka Nishiyama.

The brochure for the first PKA National Karate Championships, on July 15, 1978, featured Bill Wallace at his best.

Karate expert, Bob Wall, delivers a vicious kick to an attacker in Bruce Lee's **Game of Death**, released in 1978. *Courtesy of B. Wall*

## The 1970s

David Carradine played four characters in the 1978 film, **Circle of Iron**. Conceived by Bruce Lee and James Coburn, the film was originally titled, **Silent Flute** and was going to star Lee. Carradine was originally offered the part of the main character, Cord (played by Jeff Cooper), but preferred the multiple roles that Lee was going to play. Karate champion Joe Lewis doubled Cooper in many of the marital arts sequences.

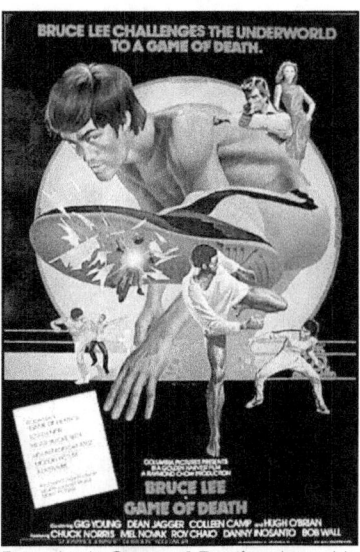

Bruce Lee's **Game of Death**, released in 1978, was put together by using a number of doubles to play Bruce, but the fight footage with the real Bruce was spectacular, and kept Lee's name alive with his fame everywhere. *Courtesy Columbia Pictures*

Peter Sellers, playing the role of Inspector Clouseau, introduces Ed Parker to the art of the shinai in **Revenge of the Pink Panther** released in 1978.

Mary Townsley, one of America's top martial arts photo-journalists, is seen here at the 1978 USKA Grand Nationals with Mike Genova (left) and Keith Vitali. *Courtesy of Mary Townsley*

Four American karate champions in 1978 (l-r): Mike Genova, Keith Vitali, Richard Jackson, and Bobby Tucker.

An Illustrated History Of Martial Arts In America – 1900 to Present

In December of 1979, Graciella Casillas (left), became the first female world champion of professional full contact karate, when she defeated Irene Garcia.

**Zen in the Martial Arts**, by Joe Hyams, became one of the best selling books on the subject in the U.S. and made Hyams a highly visible figure within the martial arts community. It was published in 1979.

One of the world's great karate masters, Mas Oyama, reveals his personal philosophy and how it has helped him reach prominence in the martial arts world. It was published in 1979 and was widely read by American marital artists of all styles.

The original founders of the Diamond Nationals in 1978 (l-r): Gary Haestilow, Larry Carnahan, Pat Worley, John Worley and Gordon Franks. *Courtesy of Larry Carnahan*

In 1979, this **Ripley's Believe It Or Not** illustration was featured world-wide. *Courtesy of George Dillman*

The 1970s

Some of the greatest fighters of the late 1970s are lined up at a major tournament in 1979. Left to right: Keith Vitali, Dan Anderson, Ray McCallum, Herb Johnson, John Longstreet, Mike Genova and Larry Kelly.   *Courtesy of K. Vitali*

In the low budget action film, **Kill the Golden Goose** (1979), famous Hapkido master Bong Soo Hahn takes on Kenpo master Ed Parker (on the ground). The film shows off Ed Parker's superb Kenpo skills, as well as Bong Soo Hahn's Hapkido prowess.

An Illustrated History Of Martial Arts In America – 1900 to Present

At the 1979 Fort Worth Nationals, Keith Vitali's team lines up (l-r): Tony Bell, Mike Genova, Keith Vitali, David Deator, and Larry Kelly. *Courtesy of K. Vitali*

Famous karate expert, Richie Barathy, demonstrated his incredible breaking skills on numerous T.V. shows during the 1970s. He's seen here with Johnny Carson on **The Tonight Show** on April 4, 1979, where he broke 13 concrete slabs while they were on fire. His sleeve caught fire and he received first and second degree burns on his arm.

In 1979 and 1980, Karen Shepherd was ranked America's number one female form competitor. In 1980, she became the first woman to win the U.S. Open Grand championship title, defeating both men and women.

The 1970s

Chuck Norris went from champion to stardom in his second film for American Cinema, **Force of One**. In the film Norris competes against full contact champion Bill Wallace who made his debut in the film, which was released in 1979. Courtesy of American Cinema

Roger Moore playing James Bond 007, fights a kendo master in the 1979 film Moonraker Courtesy of United Artists

An Illustrated History Of Martial Arts In America – 1900 to Present

Al Tracy is an American karate pioneer who in 1965 began to franchise karate schools. A Kenpo stylist, he and his brother Jim formulated the Tracy Business Systems and were the first to teach American instructors proper business practices for success. The Tracy karate schools were the largest chain in the U.S. during the 1970s. *Courtesy of A. Goldberg*

Ken Min is one of the most respected martial arts leaders in the U.S. A black belt in taekwondo (9th dan), hapkido, judo and kendo, Min became a professor at U.C. Berkley in 1969 where he oversaw the university's large martial arts program. It was mostly through his efforts that, in 1974, the AAU recognized taekwondo as a sport, and he later founded USA Taekwondo, the governing body of the sport in the U.S.

Jim Arvanitis is a Greek-American martial artist who is noted for his skill in the ancient Greek fighting art of pankration. He is the founder of his own eclectic fighting style called Mu Tau.

Texas karate champion Ray McCallum was one of the best semi-contact karate fighters in the U.S. Heralded as one of the greatest fighters of his era (1975-1990) McCallum also became a champion in full contact karate. One of the great crowd pleasers, he continually got the spectators to their feet hollering and cheering. *Courtesy of J. Beasley*

When **Taekwondo Strikes** filmed in 1974, it starred master Jhoon Rhee as a Korean Nationalist who struggles against Japanese invaders during World War II. This was the first film in the U.S. to showcase taekwondo.

# The 1980s

    This decade began with the "ninja craze". With numerous movies exalting the superhuman skills of the ninjas, Americans became "ninja crazy". Magazines wrote about it, instructors taught it and the films made big money with it. Martial artists like Chuck Norris, Jean Claude Van Damme and Steven Seagal became movie stars, as Hollywood continued to grind out martial arts movies. Movies like **Karate Kid** became mega hits.
    During this decade, full contact karate also became more popular. By the end of the decade, dojos were losing their adults, but gaining kids, who wanted to be ninjas or emulate the Karate Kid.
    By the mid 1980s, the Filipino arts were also getting some exposure, as a few masters began to teach these arts to the general public. Overall, Americans were constantly exposed to the arts through movies, television and the numerous magazines that filled the newsstands.
    Martial arts supply companies, such as Century and Asian World, began to dominate that industry. Panther Video revolutionized the martial arts world – everyone could now view the great martial artists in the privacy of their homes.

# An Illustrated History Of Martial Arts In America – 1900 to Present

In 1980, Japanese aikido and sword master, Toshishiro Obata (right) moved to the West Coast of the United States. A former member of the Tokyo Wakahoma (martial arts experts specializing in Japanese television and movie work) he soon became one of the most recognizable experts in the United States of authentic Samurai Sword Fighting and traditional weapons arts.

Tokey Hill became the first American Karate competitor to win the WUKO Karate Championships in 1980.

Paulie Zink is one of America's premier kung fu experts. He is a master of the Monkey style, which is one of the most unusual styles within the Chinese Martial Arts. Zink was also a top competitor, winning over 100 tournaments from 1970-1983, and is also a renowned weapons expert.

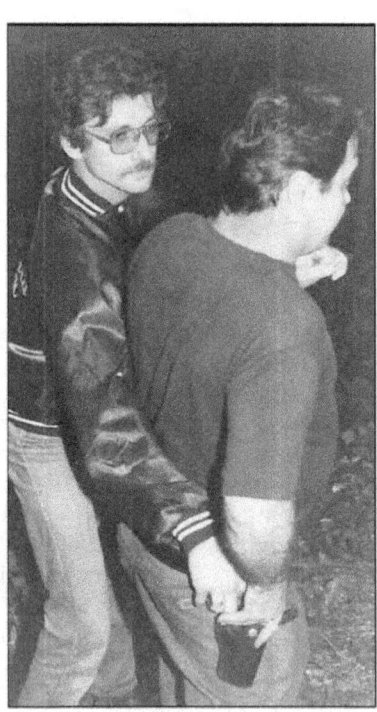

Rick Shanahan assisting the famous weapons expert/martial artist Rick Wiggington while teaching New York police officers in 1980.

## The 1980s

Bill "Superfoot" Wallace was noted for his great left-footed kicks. Here he is attempting a sidekick on world champion Ernest Hart (left) in 1980.

A group of instructors gather for the first meeting of the International Kempo Karate Association of New England in December, 1984. (L-r) Leo Lacerte, Charles Baroody, Chris Banon, Steve Solin, Don Rodriguez, Nick Cerio, Jeff Tucker, Rocky Dinco, Grey Silva, Nancy Cerio, Tony Cogliandro, Tony Pelletier.

Dr. AnnMaria (Rousey) DeMars won the World Judo Championship in 1984. She was the first American woman to win a World Judo Championship. *Courtesy of Dr. AnnMaria DeMars*

An Illustrated History Of Martial Arts In America – 1900 to Present

Pete "Sugarfoot" Cunningham is one of America's greatest full contact karate fighters. He is a W.K.A. Lightweight World Champion, and holds numerous other world titles from various sanctioning bodies. He has fought worldwide, defeating champions from Thailand, England, France, Japan and Mexico. Since 1980 he has been one of the greatest technicians in kickboxing.

Although the Brazilian art of Capoeira was introduced to the United States in the 1980s, it has, so far, not achieved a large following.

The great success of the T.V. miniseries, **Shogun**, in 1980, created a new wave of interest by Americans in the "Samurai Arts". Instruction in Iaido and Iai-Jutsu increased drastically and a number of Americans traveled to Japan to seek out instruction with well-known masters.

Best selling novel **The Ninja** by Eric Van Lustbader was published in 1980 and helped propel the "Ninja Craze" that hit the American martial arts community.

The 1980s

Keith Vitali (left) accepts the first place trophy at the 1980 AKA Nationals. During the late 1970s and early '80s, Vitali was consistently ranked the No. 1 point fighter in the country. Standing next to Keith is Sharkey and Steve Fisher. *Courtesy of K. Vitali*

In the early 1980s, dozens of low budget martial arts movies were flooding the theatres and late night TV. This eventually killed martial arts movie production for a number of years.

Due to the large number of martial arts-oriented movies being made in the 1980s, many actresses, like K.C Winkler, began to train in karate and stunt fighting.

Chicago's Fred Degerburg, who operates one of the largest (13,000 square feet) martial arts schools in the U.S., was among the first American martial artists to promote cross training. At the Degerburg Academy, in operation since 1980, students can study karate, boxing, kickboxing, jeet kune do, taekwondo, aikido, kali, muay thai and various weapons systems. *Courtesy of Jerry Beasley*

By 1980, full contact karate was firmly established in America and numerous non-contact fighters, such as Cecil Peoples (right), tried their hand at the new sport. Only a handful became successful.

By the 1980s, the Filipino martial arts were getting exposure, thanks to people like Danny Inosanto and books like these. This book was published in 1980.

Black Belt Hall of Fame member Stephen Hayes was undoubtedly one of the best-known American Ninjutsu experts during the 1970s and 1980s. A student of Ninja master Masaaki Hatsumi, Hayes promoted the art widely and became one of the most visible martial artists during the 1980s. In 1997, he founded Toshin Do, a martial art of mind and body self-protection systems based on ancient Ninja martial arts principles and updated for application to modern threats and pressures.

Since the early 1980s, Wally Jay (left), George Dillman (center) and Remy Presas were among the leaders in teaching seminars all across the country. In constant demand, the "big three" gave seminars together for over 20 years, each teaching his specialty: Jay (Ju-Jitsu), Dillman (Ryu Kyu Kempo), and Presas (modern arnis).
*Courtesy of George Dillman*

The 1980s

A group of American martial arts leaders meet in Las Vegas in 1980, prior to a full contact karate match. (L-r) Al Weiss, Curtis Wong, Chuck Norris, Emil Farkas, Stewart Sobel, Mike Stone, George Waite and Howard Hanson.

In March, 1980, Hollywood opened the first Bruce Lee Museum dedicated to the Little Dragon. Located near Hollywood and Vine, and founded by Norman Borine, the museum's 2,000 square feet contained thousands of photos, books, magazines posters and various Bruce Lee memorabilia.

Asian superstar Jackie Chan made his American film debut in the 1980 film **The Big Brawl**. The film, set in the 1930s, was a disappointing role for Chan, who returned to Hong Kong where he continued his stardom. HB Haggerty (right of Jackie Chan) was a professional football player as well as a professional wrestler.

Thanks mostly to the efforts of Rusty Kanakogi the first women's world judo championships took place in New York in November 1980.

An Illustrated History Of Martial Arts In America – 1900 to Present

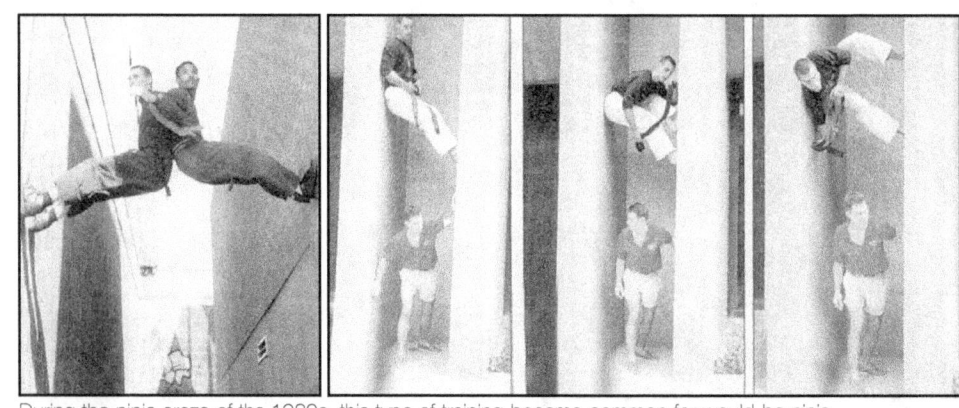

During the ninja craze of the 1980s, this type of training became common for would-be ninja.

Below, the U.S. women's team, selected for the first Women's World Judo Championships, that was held on November 28 and 29, 1980, in New York City.

L-r: Lyne Lewis, Monica Emerson, Betty Stamm and Mary Lewis.

L-r: Christine Penick, Amy Koblin, Margaret Castro, Barbara Fest and Rusty Kanakogi (coach).

The film **Force Five** was one of the first Martial arts features to include a number of top notch black belts in leading roles. The cast included (l-r) Sonny Barnes, Richard Norton, Joe Lewis, Benny Urquidez and Pam Huntington. Hapkido master Bong Soo Hahn played the lead villain. The film was directed by Robert Clouse.   *Courtesy of American Cinema*

In 1980, World Kick Boxing Champion Benny "The Jet" Urquidez got to show off his acting and martial arts skills in the film, **Force Five**. Urquidez continued to work in Hollywood, mostly in the role of a fight coordinator. In the 1990s, Benny opened one of the first film fighting classes in Hollywood.

## The 1980s

One of the biggest and most famous judo dojos in the U.S. during the 1980s was the Ishikawa Judo School in Virginia Beach, run by world-renowned sensei Takahiko Ishikawa.

George Alexander is one of the leading Shorin Ryu karate instructors in the U.S. He is also a noted Kobudo instructor, and was a top AAU karate champion. A noted historian, he has written a number of books and, today, runs his own martial arts supply and publishing company.

In 1980 Chuck Norris beat out everyone in Hollywood when he incorporated the mask wearing shadow warriors, the ninjas, in his movie **The Octagon**. The ninja craze did not begin until a year later with Cannon Films' release of **Enter the Ninja**. In **The Octagon**, Norris plays Scott James, an American who has a Ninja past and a Ninja brother that wants to kill him someday. Leading karate and weapons expert, Tadashi Yamashita, plays the role of Norris' estranged blood brother.

Cezar Borkowski was not just one of Canada's premier karate competitors but is also one of the most talented business-men in the karate world. He was one of NASKA's top kata champions in the 1980s and was the first competitor to make the bo popular in open competition. He began teaching in 1972 and presently runs a chain of very successful schools in Toronto, where he is one of the most respected names in Canadian martial arts. He teaches Shotokan.  *Courtesy of D. Warrener*

An Illustrated History Of Martial Arts In America – 1900 to Present

The West Coast Demo Team, led by Ernie Reyes (white gi, center) became the most popular demo team in the United States during the 1980s. One of the team's major attractions was Ernie Reyes Jr. (front) who, at a very young age, was a master technician and was incredible to watch. The group traveled all over the world and are still going strong today.

By 1980, full contact karate was gaining popularity as more and more events were promoted and televised. Here, Richard Jackson (left) vs Jerry Blank at the 1980 Battle of Atlanta.

Japanese superstar Toshiro Mifune, co-starred with Richard Chamberlain in the NBC-TV twelve hour epic **Shogun**, based on the best selling book by James Clavell. This 1980 Emmy winning production exposed America's martial artists to the history and traditions of feudal Japan, from which many of the martial arts originated. It was telecast over five consecutive nights from September 15-19, 1980. *Courtesy of NBC Television*

The 1980s

Canadian born Pat McCarthy (shown, choking opponent) is one of the leading historians on Okinawan karate. A former top forms and weapons champion during the 1980s, today McCarthy travels worldwide teaching and lecturing. On the left is Shito-ryu master T. Hayashi and, on the ground kicking up, is Ray Dalke.  *Courtesy of Bill Bly*

Bob Duggan (right) a Hwarang-do black belt, is the founder of Executive Security International (ESI), the oldest and most prestigious school for VIP protection, it is located in Aspen. He is seen here with Steve Biglow (left) and Fred Degerberg. *Courtesy of Fred Degerberg*

Noted not only as a top traditional karate tournament in the U.S., the "Ozawa Cup", held yearly in Las Vegas since 1981, is also noted for the world renown senseis that come to hold seminars here. L-r: F. Demura, Y. Ajari, H. Kanazawa, O. Ozawa (tournament founder) T. Hayashi and T. Mikami.

Dale Kirby is one of the leading samurai sword experts in the U.S., who was a former weapons champion during the late 1970s and early '80s.  *Courtesy of Marry Townsley*

# An Illustrated History Of Martial Arts In America – 1900 to Present

Australian-born karate and weapons expert, Ken Norton, has used his martial arts skills to become a movie star. Since moving to America, he has starred in numerous films and works with the likes of Jackie Chan, Chuck Norris and Cynthia Rothrock. He's seen here in **Force Five**.

During the 1970s and 1980s, top American martial artists were drawn to Hollywood. If they couldn't make it as actors, they often got a chance to work as stunt men or as fight choreographers. In this photo, U.S. karate champion, Mike Stone (in white) rehearses a fight scene for Cannon Films' **Enter the Ninja**. Stone, who wrote the original story for the film, was to be the original star but was replaced by Franco Nero. Stone became the film's fight coordinator and double for Nero.

Osamu Ozawa was a leading Shotokan instructor in Japan when he immigrated to the United States in 1964. One of the highest ranking Japanese Senseis in the U.S., he opened a dojo in Las Vegas in 1981 and that same year, began promoting a Traditional Karate Tournament which became one of the largest tournaments in the United States. He passed away in 1998.

The first Ninja movie by Cannon Films was **Enter the Ninja** released in 1981. The film starred Franco Nero as a ninja master, and was choreographed by American Karate champion Mike Stone, who is seen here dressed in the white ninja outfit, doubling for Nero. This movie started the ninja craze of the 1980s. *Courtesy of Cannon Films*

Sony Onowa, one of America's top kata performers, at the 1980 AKA Nationals. *Courtesy of Mary Townsley*

George Chung (extreme right) and John Chung (next to him) were two of the greatest form competitors in U.S. martial arts. They were consistently battling it out for first place in the early '80s. Far left is Karen Shepherd, also one of the all time greats of the 1980s. They are seen here at the 1981 Diamond Nationals. *Courtesy of Larry Carnahan*

Keith Vitali, with a trophy that seems heavier then he, at the 1980 AKA Nationals in Chicago. *Courtesy of Mary Townsley*

The 1980s

Sho Kosugi became the best-known "Ninja Actor" in Hollywood when he appeared in numerous films with ninja themes, beginning in 1981, with **Enter the Ninja**.

The legendary Jimmy H. Woo promoting Dave Hopkins in 1981 to black belt in Kung Fu San Soo. Hopkins has spread the word on Kung Fu San Soo with his reality based martial arts.

The South African film, **Kill and Kill Again**, featured plenty of martial arts and showcased two leading martial arts champions, Stan Schmidt and Norman Robinson, both leading South African karate-ka. Released in the United States in 1981, it starred James Ryan as a martial arts champion who attempts to rescue a kidnapped scientist. L-r: Bill Flynn, Norman Robinson, Anneline Kriel, James Ryan and Stan Schmidt. Standing in the back, Ken Gampu.

An Illustrated History Of Martial Arts In America – 1900 to Present

The Trias International Society, founded in 1948, was the first Martial Arts Hall of Fame in the United States and inducted only the best from the United States Karate Association (U.S.K.A). Here members of the society honor Master Robert Trias (in the foreground) at the 1981 U.S.K.A. Grand Nationals, for his years of devotion to the martial arts. From left to right, Phillip Koeppel, Jim McLain, Al Gene Caraulia, (the empty space represents Jim Kennedy, deceased), Phil Perales, John Pachivas, Victor Moore, Robert Bowles, Melvin Wise, James Hawkes, Parker Shelton, Glenn Keeney, Bill Wallace, and Bob Yarnall. Sitting to the left of the arena is Mike Anderson of Professional Karate magazine and Linda Lee, widow of Bruce Lee.

In September of 1982, Dr. Tsuyoshi Chitose 10th (seated) founder of Chito-ryu Karate, visits with his oldest and first non-oriental student William Dometrich (left), who introduced Chito-ryu to the U.S. On the right is George Van Horne and kneeling is James Davenport.

Isshin-ryu karate expert Joseph Jenning (right) was responsible for the video martial arts craze that hit the United States in 1982, when he began his Panther Video Productions. Jennings signed some of America's leading experts to Panther and by the end of the decade, dozens of companies were copying his success. He's seen here with author Emil Farkas.

In 1982, Scott Glenn and Toshiro Mifune starred in **The Challenge**, a modern day martial arts film directed by famous director John Frankenheimer. Swords and swordplay figure prominently throughout the movie.

The 1980s

This book was one of the first novels in the U.S. to use karate as its theme. It was published in 1983.

Steve Doss, owner of Premier Martial Arts in Austin, Texas. Doss compiled a 16 win, 3 loss, 1 draw kick boxing record by 1987.

This book, published by Overlook Press in 1983, was unique in that it was based on an award-winning documentary commissioned by the BBC on the World of Martial Arts. The book explores the various fighting arts worldwide, and gives the American reader a deep insight, not only to the physical side of the martial arts, but also to the spiritual enlightenment that many achieve from it.

By the mid 1980s, instructional videotapes had replaced books as a teaching aid. Almost every well-known martial artist had their own tapes or series of tapes.

This encyclopedia, published in 1985, was the most complete reference book published in the U.S. With over 1,000 biographies and hundreds of historical photographs, authors John Corcoran and Emil Farkas created a best-seller.

In 1981, as this headline from Variety indicates, martial arts movies were becoming an accepted genre, and the major studios were all interested in getting in on the action.

An Illustrated History Of Martial Arts In America – 1900 to Present

In 1983, Ridgely Abele won the prestigious USKA World Karate Championships. He repeated the feat in 1985 and since has become one of the leading traditional martial arts instructors in the United States. One of the top Shuri-Ryu karate masters, Abele who runs a dojo in Columbia, South Carolina is also a coach for the U.S.A. Karate Federation and is a member of the Inner Council for the International Shuri-Ryu Association.

One of the most prolific Hollywood screenwriters for high budget studio martial arts movies is Mark Kamen, the originator all of the **Karate Kid** movies. He also wrote **The Transporter** as well as the Jet Li films: **Kiss of the Dragon** and **Unleashed**.

Texas fighter, Troy Dorsey, was the only person to hold world titles in both karate and boxing. He became a full contact karate champion in 1983, and a world-boxing champion in 1991.

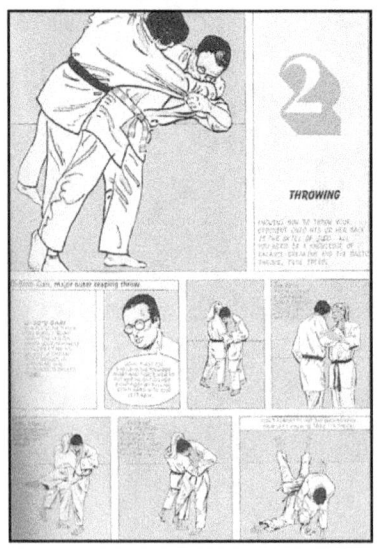

With judo's popularity Trans-world Publisher released this book in 1984, teaching judo via comic book-type drawings.

Ken Eubank is perhaps best known for the prestigious Blue Grass National Karate Tournament, which he has been promoting since 1984. A former student of Ken Knudson and Ernest Lieb, Eubank moved to Kentucky in 1979, where he became one of the area's best known and respected instructors. He was on the board of directors of NASKA. He passed away in 2006. *Courtesy of A. Goldberg*

The 1980s

With the popularity of the movie **The Karate Kid** in 1984, children flocked to karate schools all over America.

Jin Han Jae (right) is one of the most respected Korean martial arts masters in the US. Known as the "Father all of Modern Hapkido". He came to America in 1984 where he created Sin Moo Hapkido, which combines mental power with physical techniques.

In the 1983, film **Lone Wolf McQuade**, Chuck Norris stars as a maverick Texas Ranger who goes up against a vicious arms dealer, played by David Carradine. Norris shows off his plentiful martial arts talents in this movie. Norris' similarly themed T.V. show **Walker, Texas Ranger**, was inspired by this film.

By the early 1980s, full contact karate was widely practiced in the United States, and many point karate fighters tried their hand at the new sport, but only a few became successful.

1964 National Karate Champion J. Pat Burleson with his youngest son Chance, a 5th degree black belt. Oldest son Terry not pictured.

In the early 1980s, Dennis Alexio was among the leading kickboxers in the United States, and was a heavyweight world champion. In 1989, he was cast opposite Jean Claude Van Damme to play his brother, who ends up in a wheel chair at the hands of a malicious Oriental fighter, in the film **Kickboxer**.

The 1980s

Tony Anesi (right) is a leading Judo, Karate and Aiki-ju-jutsu instructor who, in 1984, was appointed Soke-dai (inheritor designate) of the Kaminshin-ryu martial arts. In 1986, he became a master instructor and his Bushido-kai dojo became the style's Hombu dojo. Today, he runs the Bushido-kai Kenyukai (Way of the Warrior Organization Research Society) and is noted for his manuals and technical articles. His dojo is located in Framingham, Mass.

It was Pat Johnson (center) who was responsible for the fight sequences of the incredibly successful Karate Kid movies. Seen with Pat are the stars Pat Morita (left) and Ralph Macchio. Courtesy of Pat Johnson

Lori Lantrip was one of America's top karate champions during the 1980s. She was adept at both fighting and forms. *Courtesy of Mike Anderson.*

Steve "Nasty" Anderson (left) was one of the top karate champions of the 1980s. He was noted for his tough, aggressive fighting style.

An Illustrated History Of Martial Arts In America – 1900 to Present

In the 1984 movie, **Missing In Action**, karate champion Chuck Norris played the role of Colonel James Braddock, a former Vietnam vet who returns to Vietnam to free a small group of American POWs still held captive there. According to Norris, he made the film as a memorial to honor his younger brother, Wieland, who was killed in Vietnam in 1970. Here, Norris is seen overpowering the sadistic Colonel Yin (Soon Tech Oh). In 1985, Norris filmed a prequel, **Missing in Action 2: The Beginning**.

Cynthia Rothrock, showing off her winning form at the 1984 LAMA Nationals in Chicago. *Courtesy of Mary Townsley*

Sho Kosugi continued his ninja exploits in this 1985 film about two anti-terrorist agents assigned to free a busload of American school children in the Philippines.

**The Karate Kid**, starring Pat Morita (right) and Ralph Macchio, hit theaters in 1984, and was a huge success. It helped rejuvenate karate and increased dojo enrollment across the country. Everyone loved the philosophy in the movie and because of this, traditional martial artists were sought out to teach, not only the physical, but also the spiritual aspects of the art.

The 1980s

World famous karate and weapons expert, Tadashi Yamashita (in center) plays the role of an evil ninja expert who runs a training camp for the villains in the film, **American Ninja** (1985).

Two of kickboxing's great champions Don Wilson (right) and Jean Yves Theriault fought it out in this event in Quebec in 1985. The match was declared a draw.

In 1984, Cannon Films released **Ninja III, the Domination**. Like other films in the genre, the hero, Sho Kosugi, has to defeat evil ninjas. In this case, a woman, Lucinda Dichey, becomes possessed by an evil ninja's spirit and only Kosugi's skill can stop her.

## An Illustrated History Of Martial Arts In America – 1900 to Present

Two great American karate champions, Lori Lautrip (left) and Linda Denley, at the AKA Nationals, 1985.
*Courtesy of Mary Townsley*

Olympic gymnastic champion, Kurt Thomas, stars in the most unusual martial arts movie ever made, called **GymKata**. It combines Thomas' superb gymnastic skills with ninja-like martial arts. Director Robert Clouse, of **Enter the Dragon**, came up with this unique American martial arts film that stands alone in the field. *Courtesy of MGM*

Famous Canadian kata champion, Jean Frenette, won the Canadian Championships ten times and competed extensively in the United States and Europe during the 1980s, when he became one of the best known karate champions in the world. He was WAKO World Champion from 1987 to 1991. His incredible kicking skills and theatrical style, performed in a traditional vein, bought him great publicity. In the mid-1980s, he began his involvement in show business and became an expert stunt performer, working on dozens of films, including **Police Academy 3** and **4**, **The Heist**, and **Highlander**.
*Courtesy of J. Frenette*

Joe Armstrong, played by Michael Dudikoff, proves his skill as a martial arts master to a skeptical Jackson (Steve James) in **American Ninja**. The two take on mercenaries in the Philippines. This Golan Globus production was released in 1985. Dudikoff went on to star in three more **American Ninja** films. *Courtesy of Cannon Films*

The 1980s

Ernie Reyes Jr., at the 1985 Diamond Nationals, competing and beating the adults. *Courtesy of Larry Carnahan*

In the 1985 MGM/UA film, **Red Sonja**, martial arts champion Ernie Reyes Jr. plays the role of a young prince who helps Brigitte Nielsen *(Red Sonja)* and Arnold Schwarzenegger track down and dispose of an evil queen. Here, Schwarzenegger holds up Ernie while Brigitte Nielsen looks on. *Courtesy of MGM/UA Films*

Taimak stars as Leroy Green, a young student of martial arts who sets out to become a master, in Berry Gordy's **The Last Dragon**, it was released in 1985. *Courtesy of Tri Star Pictures*

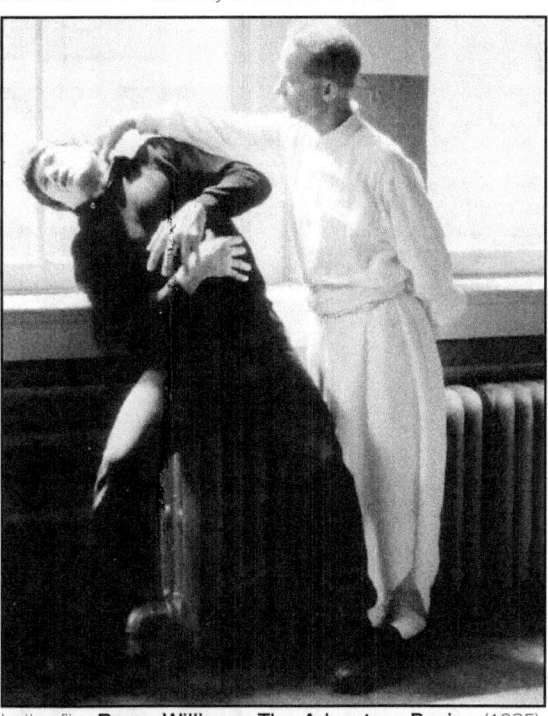

In the film **Remo Williams: The Adventure Begins** (1985), star Fred Ward, who plays a secret agent, is forced to study the mythical Korean martial art of Shinanju, from a master instructor played by Joel Grey. Here, Grey shows Ward the secrets of pressure point strikes.

# An Illustrated History Of Martial Arts In America – 1900 to Present

During the 1980s, new kicks, including the axe kick, came into play.

Two of America's leading judo men, George Harris and Takahiko Ishikawa, at a class promotion in 1986.

In 1986, **American Karate Magazine** was first published by Al Weiss. On the cover in the checkered gi is Tokey Hill, the first American WUKO World Champion. Next to him is Bonnie Taganashi, one of the East Coast's earliest female black belts. Back left is Ron Duncan, a martial arts pioneer on the East Coast.

Kurt McKeeney defeats a group of bullies in Seasonal Film's action feature **No Retreat, No Surrender**. The film, released in 1985, featured Jean Claude Van Damme in his screen debut. Star Kurt McKeeney was a legitimate black belt turned actor. *Courtesy of New World Pictures*

Martial arts action star Jean-Claude Van Damme (delivering a jump kick) got his start in the 1985 film **No Retreat, No Surrender**. In the film, Van Damme plays an evil Russian fighter named Ivan. From this movie on, Van Damme's future roles would always be heroic. *Courtesy of New World Pictures*

The 1980s

Taekwondo master Jhoon Rhee (front row, center) awarded black belts to four United States Congressmen on June 24, 1986. Directly behind Rhee is Jeff Smith. *Courtesy of J. Rhee*

Brandon Lee (Bruce Lee's son) got his first professional job in the 1986 T.V. film, **Kung Fu: The Movie**, starring David Carradine. Brandon, who is seen here twirling a three-sectional staff, played the role of Chung Wong, a Chinese Assassin.

In 1986, action star Chuck Norris decided to try his hand at comedy, in the film **Firewalker**. He, and co-star Lou Gossett Jr., play two fortune hunters in search of gold. This was Norris' first and last attempt at this genre. *Courtesy of Cannon Films*

Bruce Lee's first students, from left to right: Jesse Glover and Taky Kimura at the 1st JKD seminar in San Francisco. Professor Wally Jay is in coat and hat.

Karate champion Jean Frenette (left) played a martial arts instructor in the comedy feature, **Police Academy 3: Back in Training** (1986). He has incorporated his martial arts skills in dozens of films since then.

# An Illustrated History Of Martial Arts In America – 1900 to Present

Back to front: Charlie Mattera and Paul Taylor. Charlie Mattera, former United States Treasury Agent and founder of United Studios of Self Defense.

In 1986, David Carradine (right) reprised his role of Kwai Chang Caine in the T.V. movie, **Kung Fu: The Movie**. Already famous for his **Kung Fu** series, this time Carradine takes on an evil Manchu warlord, played by Mako. Here, Carradine is seen with Brandon Lee, who plays an evil assassin. *Courtesy of Warner Brothers Television*

With the introduction of martial arts videotapes in the 1980s, at-home study courses began to appear. Some organizations even allowed students to test for rank by sending in a homemade videotape of themselves.

Ernie Reyes Jr. starred with Gil Gerard in the 1986-87 T.V. series **Side Kicks**. In the series, which lasted for two seasons, Ernie played a karate kid who teams up with policeman Sgt. Jake Rizo (Gil Gerard) to fight crime in Southern California. The series was a big boon to the martial arts industry and got many children involved in studying the arts. *Courtesy of ABC Television*

## The 1980s

Judo great, Gene Le Bell, interviews the "Urquidez Brothers", all top black belts, at a full contact event in the 1980s. From left to right: Arnold, Blinky Rodriguez, Rubin, Benny, Manuel and Smiley.

Shaolin Kenpo karate instructor, Fred Villari, was one of the first American martial artists to franchise karate schools. In his prime, Villari had hundreds of schools across the country and produced many black belts who went on to open their own chains nationwide.

American kickboxing champion, Don "the Dragon" Wilson, catapulted his martial arts skills into Hollywood stardom when he starred in the 1989 film **Bloodfist**. The film's success led to a series of sequels and, since then, Wilson has starred in over two dozen films. Beginning his kickboxing career in 1974, Wilson, by the end of the 1980s, had won 10 world titles in 3 different weight divisions. He has been called the highest rated kickboxer of all time.

Frank Trejo (left) is one of the leading Kenpo instructors in the United States. One of Ed Parker's top students, he was an amateur and professional kickboxer and, throughout his fighting career, he has captured over 400 championships. He is the creator of "Kenpo Fusion" which combines boxing, kickboxing, karate, judo and ground fighting.

By the mid 1980s, many large professional dojos, like the one seen here, were opening up all over the United States. These full time martial arts schools were open most of the day and many had hundreds of students. A good instructor could now make a nice living. By the late 1990s, chain schools were opening up, especially on the West and East coasts.

Lisa Sliva was one of the early American female karate black belts who advocated that women learn to fight back. She gained fame when she became national director of the Guardian Angels in the 1980s and wrote books on women's self defense. Because of her high visibility, she had a great influence on women getting into the martial arts.

American traditional karate students consistently flock to seminars held by prominent karate masters, like the one held here by Shotokan sensei Hirokazu Kanazawa in the mid-1980s.

Charlie Lee, a student of famed forms champion John Chung, became a top champion himself when Chung retired in the mid-1980s. Courtesy of L. Carnahan

## The 1980s

American karate instructor and administrator Joe Mirza, who got his black belt in Shotokan karate in 1971, is the person most responsible for making the AAU karate program the largest amateur program in the U.S. Besides being the chairman of the AAU karate, Mirza also runs his own Traditional Karate-do Organization. He is based out of Chicago.

Don Rodriguez from Rhode Island is one of America's greatest karate coaches. Besides teaching his wife, three-time WAKO champion Christine Bannon Rodriguez, his team dominated the WAKO world championships for years. Rodriguez is also a first-rate promoter, running his prestigious Ocean State Championships since 1981. He is also the coach of the world-famous Paul Mitchell Karate Team.

In 1986, Chuck Merriman founded the Atlantic World Karate Team, which was the first paid professional karate team in the U.S. Made up of some of the greatest American martial artists, the team competed worldwide until 1991 and was virtually undefeated. Among its members were: Tokey Hill, Billy Blanks, Linda Denley, Cheryl Nance, Terry Creamer, Richard Plowden, Ho Sung Pak, Kevin Thompson, Chip Wright, Keith Hirabayashi, Lilly Merriman, Nasty Anderson, Christine Bannon, Alice Chang and Jean Frenette.

### Defending your life

Due to the large number of attacks against women, many high schools and colleges began to offer practical self-defense courses for their female students and faculty beginning in the mid-1980s. Newspaper articles nationwide encouraged women to learn to fight back and dozens of programs like Model Mugging was developed specifically for women

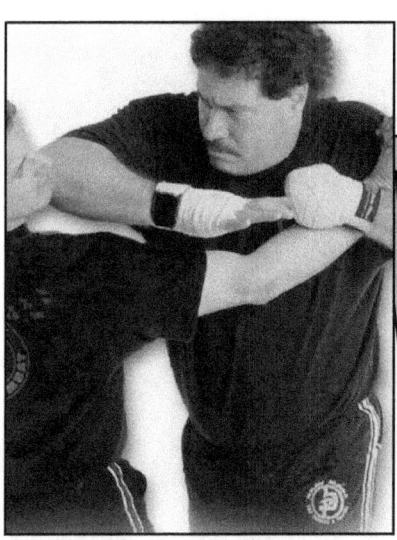

Darren Levine seen here (Rt) introduced the Israeli self-defense system of Krav Maga to the U.S. in 1982. Based on the techniques learned by the Israeli armed forces this combat oriented martial art became extremely popular and by the late 1990's it was being taught all over the U.S.

**Bloodsport**, released in 1988, made Jean-Claude Van Damme a Hollywood star. In this film about a secret contest where the world's greatest fighters battle it out in the ring – often to the death – Van Damme shows off his great kicking skills, which helped make this film a huge boxoffice success.

# An Illustrated History Of Martial Arts In America – 1900 to Present

The 1980s saw Tai Chi becoming popular with younger practitioners and university campuses often offered courses to students both as a form of exercise and a means of stress release.

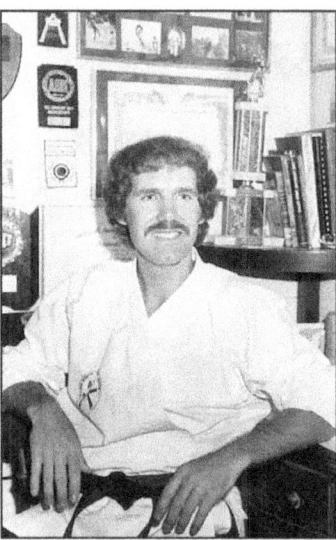

Dr. Jerry Beasley, a college professor at Redford University, Virginia, is one of the top martial arts educators in the United States. His Redford University martial arts course is nationally famous, as is his karate college martial arts camp, which exposes students to some of the greatest martial arts masters in the world. Originally a Korean stylist, he later became one of Joe Lewis' top students.

By the mid-1980s, dojos all over the country were offering special karate classes for women who wanted to learn self-defense and keep in shape.

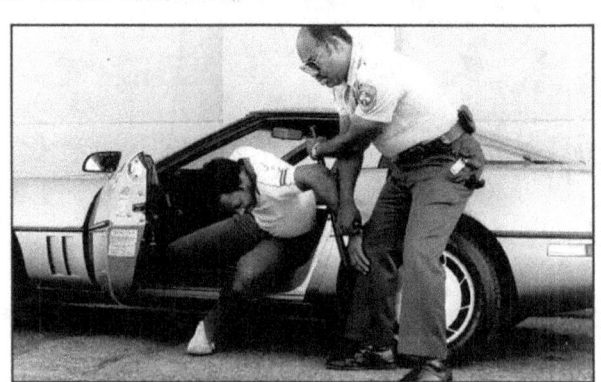

By the 1980s, many American police personnel were being trained in the use modern version of old Okinawan weapons, such as the tonfa seen here.

Century began producing martial art products in 1976 and is today recognized as the largest supplier of martial arts products in the world. Century moved to its new location in Midwest City, Oklahoma in 1982.

# The 1980s

By the 1980s, hundreds of women black belts were competing regularly at tournaments. Many women who were not too keen on fighting would compete in the kata division.

Jean-Yves Theriault, a Canadian martial artist, became the world middleweight kickboxing champion on November 15, 1980. He quickly became a superstar in Canada and, during the 1980s, was one of the best-known martial arts figures in North America. He retired in 1995 undefeated.

By the 1980s, breaking competition became commonplace at many of America's karate tournaments.

WAKO World Karate Champion John Chung was one of America's leading tournament competitors in the 1980s. A leading kata champion, he won almost every major tournament in the early 1980s and was named to the Black Belt Hall of Fame in 1982 as the 'Forms Competitor of the Year'. In 1980, John, with his sister Helen, performed a martial ballet, which won second place on the nationally syndicated T.V. show Dance Fever. He was a protégé of Jhoon Rhee.

## An Illustrated History Of Martial Arts In America – 1900 to Present

In November of 1980, the U.S. team went to the 5th World Karate Championships (WUKO) and came back with a gold medal won by Tokey Hill (standing, 2nd from left). He was the first American WUKO World Champion. The team coach was Chuck Merriman (standing, 10th from left)

Cynthia Rothrock was one of America's top female kata and weapons competitors during the 1980s. She was consistently ranked number one until 1985 when Rothrock began a film career in the Hong Kong based film **Yes, Madame**. With over 30 films to her credit, Rothrock has become the leading female martial arts star in the world. *Courtesy of C. Rothrock*

The Filipino art of Arnis and Kali invaded America in the early 1980s. By the mid-1980s, it was widely practiced. Remy Presas, the "Father of Modern Arnis", came to the United States in 1975 and has been extremely instrumental in spreading the art.

The 1980s

In the 1980s, Dennis Brown became one of the best kung-fu champions competing on the American karate circuit. He was one of the first American martial artists to study in China, and, is today, one of the most accomplished non-oriental kung fu experts in America.

Billy Blanks, seen here defeating William Oliver, was one of the top karate fighters in the United States during the 1980s.

Hawaiian-born Ted Tabura is one of the leading martial arts instructors in Southern California. An expert in the Lima Lama style of karate and in Kajukempo, Tabura became famous for his demonstration teams that were spectacular, especially with weapons. He promotes the Festival of Kings Karate Championships in Maui, Hawaii.

Benny "the Jet" Urquidez (above, right) was one of the first American kickboxers to successfully challenge and defeat Thai boxers, even on their home turf. He has won six World Championships in five weight divisions.

## An Illustrated History Of Martial Arts In America – 1900 to Present

Although the first official demonstration of Thai kickboxing (Muay Thai) in the U.S. occurred in 1962 at the Seattle World Fair, it wasn't until the 1980s that the sport gained some popularity in the U.S., due mostly to the interest in kickboxing and full contact karate.

By the 1980s, traditional weapon training became common at many karate dojos. The most common weapon taught at many schools was the bo (staff). Here, a class goes through a basic drill at a traditional dojo.

Charlie Mattera (left), founder of the United Studios of Self Defense with the legendary Nick Cerio (right), his instructor. Mattera has created over 1500 martial arts studios in the United States.

American karate champion, Keith Vitali, made his screen debut in Cannon Films, **Revenge of the Ninja**. This film released in 1983 starred Sho Kosugi, who takes on the evil ninja, played by Eric Roberts.

The 1980s

Steven Plinck (left) is a top-notch Silat instructor and is recognized as one of the most senior practitioners of Serak in America. He is seen here with Fred Degerburg (center) and John DeJong. *Courtesy of Fred Degerberg*

Fred Degerburg (left) with Escrima master Lucay Lucay.

Robert Bussy, who began training in the martial arts in his early teens, was running the largest ninja training facility in the world by 1984. A 12,000 sq. foot facility in Omaha, Nebraska, this "Ninja College" attracted students from all over the U.S and overseas. An unorthodox instructor, Robert Bussey's Warrior International (RBWI) had thousands of students during the American Ninja craze of the '80s. In 1997, Bussey disbanded his organization.

By the mid 1980s, many martial artists discovered that bodyguarding could be a lucrative profession. Numerous black belts even opened their own security agencies, specializing in "Black Belt Security".

An Illustrated History Of Martial Arts In America – 1900 to Present

Kung fu expert, Tat-Mau Wong,, is one of the most influential Chinese martial artists in the United States. Since he opened his Choy Lay Fut Kung Fu Institute in San Francisco, in 1983, he has been attempting to make Chinese Martial Arts popular and respectful. For this reason, he organized the first All Chinese Martial Arts Championships in 1987. Currently, he is the Vice President of the U.S.A. Wushu Kung Fu Federation.

Rick Rufus (left) connects to the head of John Mancayo. In April of 1987, Rufus became the youngest World Middleweight Champion in full contact karate history when he knocked out Mancayo in the seventh round with a short left hook to the chin.

Exotic martial arts, such as Krabi Krabong, were beginning to be practiced in the United States by the mid-1980s. Alfonso Tamez (right) was one of the foremost instructors of this Thai combat system.

Aikido, which has been practiced in the United States since the 1960s, really didn't become popular until 1988. This was the year when aikido expert, Steven Seagal, starred in the film, **Above the Law** and showed off his aikido skill.

By 1988, Chuck Norris was a big Hollywood star, so with the help of famous author, Joe Hyams, Norris wrote his life story, as well as his personal philosophy that has led him to reach fame and fortune.

The 1980s

Kathy Jones, a Shito Ryu stylist, was one of the foremost American traditional kata competitors during the 1980s. She was ranked internationally as one of the best in the world.

One of the first books to demonstrate how the martial arts could be applied in the business world. Published in 1988.

Sam Kuoha became the inheritor of William K.S. Chow's kara-ho kempo karate system, after Professor Chow's death in 1987.

In 1987, U.S. judo champion, Mike Swain, became the first American to win the coveted gold medal in the World Judo Championships. He was also a Bronze medalist at the 1988 Olympics in Seoul, Korea. Swain, who began judo at age 8, has been five times National Champion and four times National College Champion. In 1996, he was chosen as the Men's Olympic Judo Coach.

An Illustrated History Of Martial Arts In America – 1900 to Present

In 1987, Michael Dudikoff starred in **American Ninja 2 – The Confrontation** *(above and left)*. This was a follow up to his earliest **American Ninja** film, which he made in 1985. *Courtesy of Cannon Films*

In 1988, aikido in America got a major boost when Steven Seagal used his aikido skill in the film **Above the Law**. Seagal, an aikido expert who trained in Japan, got Americans into Aikido dojos all over the country.

In 1988, Dana Hee took home a gold medal for the United States when she won the Olympic gold medal in Tae Kwon do in Seoul, Korea. Dana later moved to Los Angeles to pursue a career in movies and television.

The 1980s

Martial arts action star, Sho Kosugi, starred in the 1987 film **Rage of Honor**. Like in his previous movies, Kosugi shows off his superb martial arts skills as he battles drug dealers in Argentina.   *Courtesy of MGM*

One of the reasons Jean-Claude Van Damme became so successful in martial arts movies was his incredible flexibility, which he demonstrates here.

Reality based self defense training, especially for the women, became popular during the late 1980s, due to the huge crime rate and to the numerous self-defense courses that women could take. Even many high schools were beginning to offer self-defense classes to their senior students.

Jimmy Kim, who began training in taekwondo in 1969 with his father, became the senior United States National Champion in 1985, 1987 and 1988 and, the same year, became a Gold medalist at the Seoul Olympics.

Arlene Limas was a top karate competitor on the open karate circuit before getting involved with Olympic Taekwondo in 1986. In 1988, she won a gold medal at the Seoul Olympics.

An Illustrated History Of Martial Arts In America – 1900 to Present

Actor Sam Jones "Flash Gordon" in the 1983 US National Top Ten Karate Championships promoted by Leo Fong and Ron Marchini.

During the late 1980s and early '90s, Kathy Long, five time World Female Kickboxing Champion was the best known female martial artist in the United States. She was featured on the cover of every martial arts publication and numerous mainstream magazines ran articles about her.

Taekwondo and Hapkido expert Phillip Rhee is not only a top martial artist but an actor director and producer who has created the famous **Best of the Best** martial arts film series. Beginning in 1989 with the first **Best of the Best**, Rhee has over seen three more sequels. He not only acted in all of them, but he directed **Best of the Best 3** (1995) and **Best of the Best 4** (1998).

Morio Higaonna, one of the world's leading experts on Okinawan Goju-ryu karate, moved to San Diego in 1989 where he headquartered his International Goju-ryu Karate Federation (IOGKF). Higaonna was one of the most popular demonstrators at numerous American tournaments and was also in high demand for seminars. *Courtesy of Morio Higaonna*

Michael Bernardo, from Canada, was a noted competitor during the late 1980s and early 1990s. He was especially adept at weapons, winning over 57 straight weapons divisions consecutively and was also a nationally ranked kata competitor. *Courtesy of L. Carnahan*

The 1980s

Dr. Terrance Webster Doyle is an author and a martial arts educator noted for his martial arts for peace concepts, which helps young people understand how to resolve conflict peacefully. His books continually win awards and are internationally endorsed for its attempt at teaching children peace through martial arts.

Hapkido expert Bong Soo Hahn instructs Sean Connery on how to use his fingers as deadly weapons for the film **Presidio** (1988).

In **Kickboxer**, Jean-Claude Van Damme enters the brutal world of Thai kickboxing when his brother is badly injured in a Muay Thai match and Van Damme vows to avenge him. Many claim this is the best martial arts movie Van Damme has ever made, and it certainly continued his longevity in Hollywood. It was released in 1989.
*Courtesy of Kings Road Entertainment*

An Illustrated History Of Martial Arts In America – 1900 to Present

The mid '80s saw many high schools offering self-defense classes to its senior girls, as an extracurricular activity.

Hee Il Cho (center) was one of the country's best-known taekwondo instructors and in the 1980's promoted a number of tournaments in Los Angeles. Seen here at one of his events with (left to right) Bong Soo Hann, Dexter Brooks, Cho, Alvin Prouder and Berry Gordon.

Keith Cooke Hirabayashi began his martial arts training with Roger Tung in Wushu in 1973 and, in the 1980s, traveled to China to continue his training. He began his competitive career in the early 1980s and by the mid-1980s was one of the top competitors in the country. His skills landed him a movie role in **China O'Brian** (starring Cynthia Rothrock) and, today, he works regularly in films as an actor and stuntman. He also runs his own dojo in the affluent Brentwood area of Los Angeles.

By the mid 1980s, many leading American martial artists were traveling the country giving seminars. One of the most sought after instructors was Danny Inosanto (left), a student of Bruce Lee who became the best known Jeet Kune Do instructor in the world.

# The 1990s

Kids were beginning to dominate the dojos, and no holds barred fighting arrived in 1993 with the Ultimate Fighting Championships (UFC). Taekwondo and karate were still the most widely practiced of the martial arts, but by the mid-'90s enrollment in these dojos was mostly children. Thanks to pay-per-view TV, millions of Americans were exposed to the no holds barred events and thanks to the Royce Gracie win at the first UFC, Brazilian jujutsu became extremely popular. The grappling arts were now beginning to be widely practiced again and the trend toward mixed martial arts was on the rise.

This was also the decade in which the practical, street effective, combat styles became extensively exposed. Dozens of instructors were teaching realistic fighting skills and systems like Krav Maga were on the rise.

The business of martial arts also got a boost when organizations like NAPMA began to gain popularity, as instructors wanted to, not only become better black belts, but better business people as well. Dojos were becoming bigger and more professional, and numerous well-known instructors were earning a substantial living. Thanks to Steven Seagal, aikido became much more visible and began to grow substantially.

By the end of the decade, a fair number of people were practicing arts such as tai chi, wu shu, escrima, jeet kune do, iaido, yudo and aikido. Of course, cross training became fairly common. This was also the decade that Tae Bo and executive boxing became popular, and the martial arts industry discovered a new way to entice adults into the dojo, focusing on the physical fitness side of the arts.

An Illustrated History Of Martial Arts In America – 1900 to Present

Ernie Boggs is one of the greatest sport jujitsu competitors of all time. In 1990 he was the first American to win the world championships and since has been the coach of the USA sport jujitsu team. He hosted the 1996 ISJA sport jujitsu world championships in West Virginia.

Pan Quing Fu is a Chinese martial arts master, who was one of China's youngest national champions. In 1990 he portrayed himself in the cult movie **Iron and Silk**. Today, he resides and teaches in Canada. *Courtesy of Fran Sanchez*

In 1990, Chuck Norris formed the Kick Drugs Out of America Foundation. KDOOA is a martial arts training program integrated into public school systems that aims to change young lives through education and motivation.

Former Goju-ryu black belt Jeff Speakman became one of Ed Parkers top protégés, and formed the United Kempo system after Parker passed away in 1990. Speakman began a film career in 1991 with **The Perfect Weapon**, which became the first American movie to showcase Ed Parker's kenpo system.

The 1990s

The **Teenage Mutant Ninja Turtles**, which was first seen as a cartoon series on T.V. in the late 1980s, became a big theatrical film in 1990 and was followed by a number of successful sequels. This helped rejuvenate the kids martial arts market and boosted enrollment in dojos all over the country.

**Armenian** born Judo and Sambo champion Gokor Chivichyan, moved to the United States in 1981, where he became famous for his no holds barred skills, winning 4 professional world NHB Championship titles. In 1991, he opened his own Grappling Academy in Hollywood, and many of his students have become top judo and no holds barred competitors.

A nice tribute to one of America's greatest martial artists. *Courtesy of Mary Townsley*

Brian Frost is head of the Koikan style of karate in the US. A former all Japan Koeikan karate champion (1972), Frost has trained under the styles founder Onishi Eizo for over 35 years. He is seen here with Onishi Sensei.

John De Pasqual probably runs the largest independent chain of Shotokan schools in the country, the Illinois Shotokan with over 70 locations and over 8,000 students. Headquartered in Chicago, De Pasqual a former top competitor has over 450 black belts under him. *Courtesy of Bill Bly*

Released in 1990 as a sequel to Norris' first **Delta Force** (1986) this film was directed by Chuck's brother Aaron.

An Illustrated History Of Martial Arts In America – 1900 to Present

Seven-time National Taekwondo champion Herb Perez became a Gold medalist at the 1992 Olympic games. Perez has been a United States National team captain six times and one of the best known Taekwondo practitioners in the United States. He is in constant demand as a teacher, coach, seminar leader & writer.

In January of 1992, **The Journal of Asian Martial Arts** began to be published. According to publisher Michael A. De Marco, "this quarterly journal is devoted to studies that offer better understanding of the culture from which martial arts arose and in which they continue to thrive." The journal was the first scholarly magazine in the U.S. written with mature, high academic standards.

Brandon Lee starred in the action adventure film **Rapid Fire** (1992) in which he goes up against a group of drug lords. The film, which was Brandon's first starring role, showcases his martial arts skills.

Chris Casamassa is an American martial artist, actor and stuntman who is best known for his role as Scorpion in the movie Mortal Kombat. He is the son of martial arts guru, and founder of Red Dragon Karate Louis D. Casamassa.

# The 1990s

Aikido expert and movie star Steven Seagal's biggest box office hit was the film **Under Siege** in which he played Casey Ryback, a personal cook to the captain of the battleship, Missouri. When the ship is taken over by a gang of terrorists, it is Ryback who has to stop them. This film was released in 1992 and made Seagal a big star in Hollywood. *Courtesy of Warner Brothers*

Frank E. Sanchez is noted as the founder of America's first grandmaster's council, The World of Family Sokeship Council. Founded in 1993, the council is composed of 9th and 10th dan grandmasters and their equivalents. Sanchez is also the founder of San Jitsu, which is Guam's first recognized martial arts system.

John Pellegrini, who has studied martial arts since age 12, became a black belt in Taekwondo and Hapkido.

In 1992 Americans for the first time got a chance to see the incredible feats of the Shaolin monks of China as they toured the U.S. Their incredible martial arts skills rekindled an interest in the Chinese arts.

By the early 1990s, the Filipino martial arts were getting so popular, that instructors like Danny Inosanto were constantly kept busy, traveling the U.S., and holding seminars in these arts.

Bill Ryusaki, teacher of the Urquidez clan and Cecil Peoples. A phenomenal martial arts teacher, was also known as an outstanding fight choreographer, a career spanning over four decades.

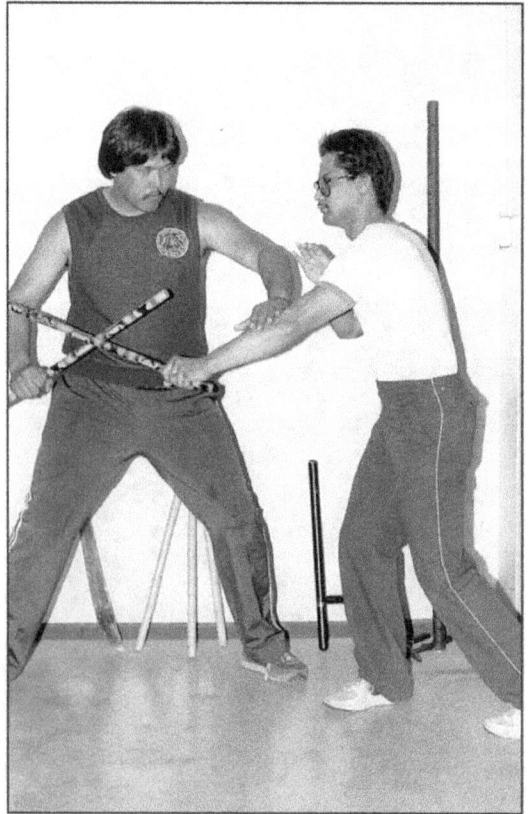

Escrima master Rene Latosa (left), is one of the most influential Filipino martial arts instructors in the United States. He studied under Angel Cabales and Maximo Sarmiento in Stockton, California, and when he joined the air force, he gave instruction to fellow servicemen. He introduced Escrima to England and to Germany and settled in San Francisco from where he continues to promote his art. He was one of the first instructors to promote Sport Escrima in the United States.

Burton Richardson is one of the world's premier Jeet Kune Do instructors. A former student of Dan Inosanto, Richardson has trained extensively in Thai Boxing, Pentyak Silat, Kali and Brazilian jiu-jitsu. Richardson writes extensively on the subject of realistic no-nonsense combat and teaches worldwide. *Courtesy of B. Richardson*

Ho Sung Pak became the first competitor in American martial arts tournament history to receive a unanimous 10-point (perfect) score from each of the judges for kata at a major tournament. The 1991 Diamond Nationals. One of the leading Wushu experts in the United States, Pak was among the top competitors nationwide during the late 1980s and early 1990s. He played Raphael in the **Teenage Mutant Ninja Turtle** movies, **II** and **III**.

The 1990s

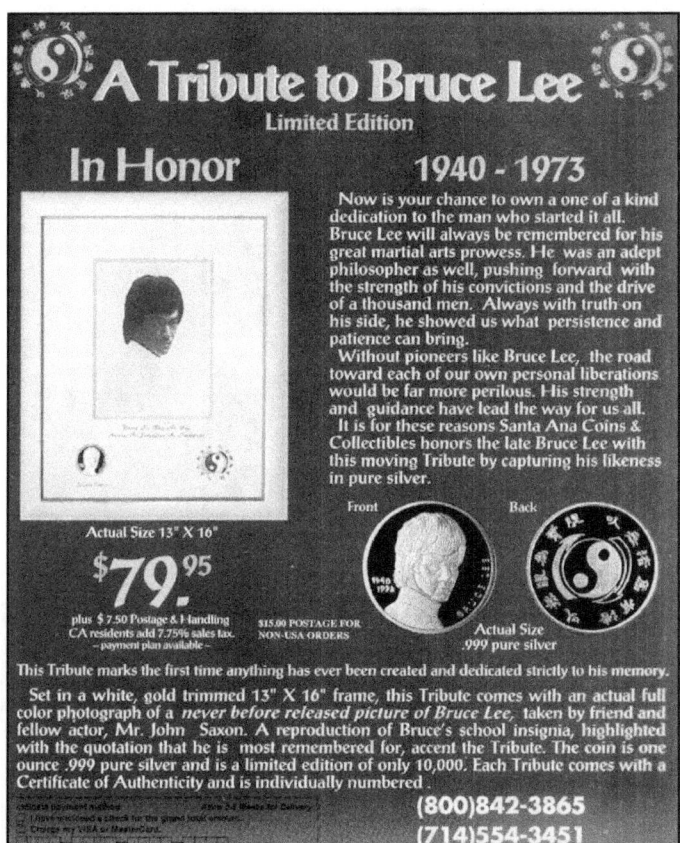

In the early '90s, Bruce Lee became the only martial artist to have a limited edition silver coin minted in his honor.

Richard Brandon was one of the leading soft-style forms competitor in the US during the early 1990s. He was among the best for over 10 years. *Courtesy of Larry Carnahan*

Jake Reynaga is a Japanese, Okinawan forms competitor on the open circuit, who has, since the early '90s been a consistent winner at all the big tournaments. *Courtesy of Larry Carnahan*

## An Illustrated History Of Martial Arts In America – 1900 to Present

In 1993, Warner Brothers Television revived the old **Kung Fu** series, but this time Kwai Chang Caine (David Carradine) is the grandson of the original Cane and is living in present day New York's Chinatown, where he helps his policeman son, Peter (Chris Potter) apprehend criminals. The series lasted until 1997. *Courtesy of Warner Brothers*

Two of the East Coast's great karate instructors Nick Cerio (left) and Don Rodriguez.

*Courtesy of D. Rodriguez*

Lorenzo Lamas, who used his martial arts skills regularly on his T.V. series **Renegade** (1992-1996) got his black belt from Burbank-based Al Thomas in 1991.

American karate champion, Chuck Norris, became a major television star when he starred in the CBS action drama, **Walker, Texas Ranger**. The show, which ran from April 21,1993-May 19, 2001, featured Norris as a contemporary Texas Ranger who uses his martial arts skills to bring down the bad guys. *Courtesy of CBS Television*

# The 1990s

The octagonal caged arena is the 'trademark of the Ultimate Fighting Championships (UFC) which had its first event on November 12, 1993, at the McNichols Sports Arena in Denver and was won by Royce Gracie. The UFC was originally started by Rorion Gracie and Art Davie. The event was an instant success, with over 86,000 pay per view subscribers. Although the UFC was sold in 1995, it continues to this day and is more popular then ever.

Ken Shamrock has become one of the best-known American mixed martial arts fighters. Originally a wrestler, he appeared in the first UFC in 1993, where he lost to Royce Gracie. He and Gracie again fought in 1995 at the first UFC "Superfight", and the match was a draw. Shamrock has won numerous titles since and still makes appearances in the UFC. He founded the Lion's Den, a famous school of submission fighting.

In 1993, Rorion Gracie (standing) created the Ultimate Fighting Championships, which was the beginning of the 'No Holds Barred' craze that followed. It was also Rorion who first introduced Brazilian Ju jitsu to the United States when he moved to southern California in 1979.

An Illustrated History Of Martial Arts In America – 1900 to Present

On May 31, 1993 Brandon Lee (Bruce's son) was fatally shot while filming **The Crow**, a gothic urban fantasy for Mirimax/Dimension Films. The death was ruled accidental and Brandon was buried next to his father in Lakeview Cemetery in Seattle. The Crow was released in 1994 and became a box office smash.

It was actor Jason Scott Lee who was chosen to portray the late Bruce Lee in the film **Dragon: The Bruce Lee Story**. The film was released in 1993 on the 20th anniversary of Lee's passing.

Royce Gracie was the winner of the first Ultimate Fighting Championships and was instrumental in introducing Brazilian Ju-Jutsu to the American public.

## The First Martial Arts Talk Radio Show...
# WARRIOR TALK®

- **WARRIOR TALK**®...the first martial arts talk radio program in martial arts history!
- Featuring internationally renowned **Martial Arts Masters**
- **Hard-hitting**, focused and factual conversation
- Learn about **Karate, Judo, Jujitsu, Tai Chi, Aikido, Tae Kwon Do** ... the list goes on and on!

"The Warrior Of the Airwaves" Dr. Aiello

Co-host Dina Baganz

### Call your local Stations and Networks for show times!

**Warrior Talk**, started in 1993, by Jerry Aiello, has featured some of the greatest names in American martial arts.

The 1990s

Jerry Beasley (right) is seen here with three of the leading martial artists in the U.S. who were teaching at his famous karate college in the mid-1990s. L-r: Bill Wallace, Benny Urquidez and Joe Lewis.

Ernie Reyes (left) starred with his son Ernie Reyes Jr. in the 1993 film **Surf Ninjas**. This fantasy film finds two teenage brothers trying to overcome a dictator of an exotic island using their martial arts skills.

On August 7, 1993, a Bruce Lee memorabilia sale in Beverly Hills fetched over three hundred thousand dollars. The personal hand written letter seen here fetched over $29,000.

In 1994, John Graden (left), seen here with his instructor Joe Lewis, founded the National Association of Professional Martial Arts (NAPMA). This organization's goal was to strengthen the professional skills of martial arts school owners. A year later, Graden launched **Martial Arts Professional Magazine** - the first journal to focus on the business side of the martial arts. In 2004, he founded the Martial Arts Teacher's Association.

An Illustrated History Of Martial Arts In America – 1900 to Present

In 1994, Russell Wong starred in the T.V. series **Vanishing Son**. Wong, a proficient martial artist, displayed his skills in each episode. The series only lasted one season.

Glen C. Wilson is a leading American kung fu expert who was a disciple of the late Daniel K. Pai, becoming one of foremost practitioners of the Pai Lum Tao system. Pai and Wilson formed the White Dragon Society in order to standardize Pai Lum Tao. Upon Pai's death in 1993, Wilson became the Society's head. Wilson was also a leading national and international competitor, winning numerous titles. He is headquartered in Florida.

Robin Shou, who portrays a warrior in the film **Mortal Combat** (1995), is a kempo and wushu expert.

The 1990s

Hilary Swank took over the lead opposite Pat Morita in **Karate Kid IV** released in 1994.

Victor de Thouars introduced pentjak silat serek, the Indonesian martial arts, to the American public when he opened his first Academy in 1994 in Bellflower, California.

One of the biggest trends in the 1990s was Brazilian Jiu-Jitsu. It seems everyone wanted to try it, and many stand up fighters began to study it.

## An Illustrated History Of Martial Arts In America – 1900 to Present

Julius Thiery (left), seen here with Hirokazu Kanazawa, has been a long-time leader in the traditional karate community. A top-notch coach and referee, in 1994 Thiery founded the USA National Karate-Do Federation, which is the governing body of sports karate. He is headquartered in Seattle.

Two great American taekwondo instructors, Jhoon Rhee (left) and Keith Yates in 1994. *Courtesy of Keith Yates*

Greg Silva is one of America's leaders in the martial arts business industry. Owner of United Professionals, he is one of the most knowledgeable martial arts business experts whose expertise is in constant demand. Mr. Silva is also a high ranking Kenpo black belt.

David "Tank" Abbott made his mixed martial arts debut in 1995 and achieved popularity because of his display of power and aggression. Many claimed his fighting style was more reminiscent of a street fighter than a martial artist.

The 1990s

Howard High, a Ryobukai karate instructor, is famous as the originator of the first cyber dojo on the web, which allows martial artists to chat to each other. *Courtesy of Bill Bly*

Shieru Takashina is one of America's leading Shotokan instructors. A member of the I.S.K.A. under Okazaki sensei, he teaches out of Florida. *Courtesy of Bill Bly*

Promoters Fred Degerberg (left), Scott Kifer and Tom Letuli present Chuck Norris with a check for over $100,000 for his Kick Drugs Out of America Foundation. The 1995 expo was held in Chicago, with over 10,000 people in attendance. *Courtesy of Fred Degerberg*

With kids' karate classes growing by leaps and bounds in the 1990s, American publishers began to offer books appealing to the young karate-ka. This book explores the subject of bullying and how a 12-year-old karate student uses his skills to avoid confrontation.

In 1996, Daniel Bernhardt (above and inset) starred in **Bloodsport II: The Next Kumite**. Bernhardt, a former male model and practicing martial artist, trained with He Il Choi (who appears in the film) for over three years, just prior to filming.

227

## An Illustrated History Of Martial Arts In America – 1900 to Present

Don Frye, who began his mixed martial arts career in 1996, was a college wrestler and holds a black belt in judo. He was one of the top American fighters defeating the likes of Ken Shamrock, David Abbott and Gary Goodridge.

In 1996, action star Steven Seagal teamed up with Keenen Ivory Wayans in the action thriller **The Glimmer Man**. In the film, a cop with an attitude (Wayans) is partnered up with a cop with a shady past and amazing martial arts skills (Seagal). *Courtesy of Warner Brothers*

By the 1990s, many martial artists with aspirations of becoming Hollywood stuntmen began studying stunt fighting, which required not only skills in fighting, but in reacting as well.

The 1990s

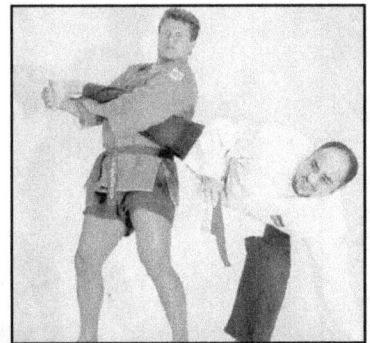

Former Russian Sambo and Judo champion, now living in the United States, Oleg Taktarov, became a top 'No Holds Barred' fighter during the 1990s. In 1999, he began a film career and, when not filming, he teaches advanced fighting classes in Southern California.

Cung Lee, a noted San Shou champion and mixed martial arts fighter, has become one of the best known martial artist in the U.S. since the mid-1990s. He is noted for his incredible scissor kick takedown, seen here, and is a big draw at all tournaments where he competes.

Mike Chat is the founder of XMA, or extreme martial arts, which became popular in the late 1990s. An expert in Okinawan Shorei ryu karate, taekwondo, wushu and acrobatics, Mike has combined all these into an extremely visual and crowd-pleasing acrobatic martial arts style. Mike has captured over 50 national and international forms and weapons championships and, since 1996, has appeared in numerous films and TV shows including the **Power Rangers**.

American karate champion Christine Bannon-Rodriguez began her training at age 13. By the mid-'90s, she was one of the country's greatest competitors. Besides winning almost every major tournament in the country, Christine was the only Triple Crown winner at the '91 and '93 WAKO World Championships. Christine, who lives in Rhode Island, is married to karate instructor and promoter Don Rodriguez. *Courtesy of D. Rodriguez*

An Illustrated History Of Martial Arts In America – 1900 to Present

Mark Dacascos was born into the martial arts with world famous Al Dacascos as his father, and Melia Bernal as his mother. A consistent tournament winner as a teenager, Mark pursued acting and has done dozens of films, in many of which he has showcased his incredible martial arts skills.

Not until the 1990s, when reality-based martial arts started becoming popular, did grappling arts like ju-jutsu become widely practiced again. Here, California based ju-jutsu expert Norm Leff works out with one of his students.

One of the newest Israeli combat systems to be taught in the U.S. is Haganah, a Hebrew word-meaning defense. It was created by Mike Kanarek, a former Israeli Special Forces operative, who began teaching it in the U.S.. around the mid-1990s.

By the 1990s, thousands of American women were achieving a black belt rank in karate and Tae Kwon Do. For most women, the primary goal of training was self-defense, followed by physical fitness.

The 1990s

Michele "Mouse" Krasnoo was one of the top female karate champions of the 1990's. Noted for her kata and weapon skills, she has won hundreds of first place titles and 48 grand championships. She is an NBL world titleholder and has lately pursued motion picture work in Hollywood.

Tom Letuli, seen here in the 1990s, with three of America's leading female karate experts (Karen Shepherd, Christine Bannon Rodriguez and Cynthia Rothrock), was among the top martial arts promoters in America. He promoted hundreds of events from tournaments, to charity events, to full contact events, mostly in the Chicago area.

During the 1990s, many adults joined karate schools, not only for self-defense training, but for the serenity and meditation that helped them cope with the pressures of every day life.

Gerald Okamura, seen here in the film **Big Trouble in Little China**, is a high-ranking black belt in Kung Fu San Soo. He is known throughout the U.S. as a designer of various types of weaponry, many of which has been featured in numerous movies. He began his acting and stunt career when he played a Shaolin monk in the T.V. series **Kung Fu** and has since played various roles in dozens of films. In 1995 Okamura began the now famous Dragon Festival, an annual event held in Southern California where renowned martial artists and Hollywood celebrities donate their time, allowing the public to meet them.

## An Illustrated History Of Martial Arts In America – 1900 to Present

John Valera was one of the greatest form competitors of the '90s. An open stylist, he began competing as a child and was an extremely talented martial artist. Combining gymnastics and karate, he retired in 1999 to pursue a career in Hollywood.
*Courtesy of L. Carnahan*

Lee Pei Jun was a former shaolin monk who became a leading competitor in the 1990s on the U.S. open karate circuit. He later went to China to work on a number of films.

By the mid 1990s, most karate dojos were made up of kids, many as young as four.

Douglas Wong is one of the best-known sifus in the U.S. A founder of the White Lotus kung fu System, Wong, who teaches in Southern California, has taught thousands of students, including numerous top competitors. He has authored a number of books on kung fu and has starred in a number of videos. In 1992, he trained Jason Scott Lee for his role in **Dragon, The Bruce Lee Story** and also instructed Kevin Sorbo who starred in TV's **Hercules**.

Jodo, though not widely practiced, became more popular during the 1990s when students discovered its effectiveness as a self-defense weapon that could be carried legally, as a cane.

## The 1990s

American karate champion Karen Shepherd began her film career in 1981 when she went to Japan to film **The Shinoki Ninja**. She is seen here in her role as the "Enforcer" in the T.V. series **Hercules: The Legendary Journeys**.

Nicky Carlson Lee (right) was among the top women fighters of the '90s. She has won the prestigious Diamond nationals eight times. Nicky retired in 2000. *Courtesy of Larry Carnahan*

By the mid-1990s, reality-based martial arts were beginning to be practiced widely. In many martial arts schools students practiced without uniforms, in street clothes and, often fought heavily padded opponents, to add realism to their techniques.

# An Illustrated History Of Martial Arts In America – 1900 to Present

Ming Lu was a top soft style and weapons champion in the mid-90s. She would consistently defeat the men in both forms and weapons and, is today, pursuing a career in Hollywood. *Courtesy of Larry Carnahan*

With the no holds barred craze in the mid-1990s, many dojos began to offer these types of classes to their students.

A leading American Karate champion during the 1970s, Billy Blanks gained worldwide fame during the 1990s when his Tae Bo, which combines dance moves and Taekwondo, became the newest physical fitness craze in America. In 1989, he moved to Los Angeles where he opened his Billy Blanks World Training Center, and numerous Hollywood celebrities became his clients. His many tapes and DVDs have become all time bestsellers.

Ninja bar for young ninjas.

The 1990s

With the children's martial arts market so huge in the 1990s, this karate coloring book was a natural.

Due to the large number of children practicing karate by the late 1990s, a photo Christmas card like this was not uncommon.

This book, written by John Graden in the 1990s, helped many good black belts to also become good businessmen.

By the mid-1990s, numerous exotic weaponry was taught in many dojos throughout the country. Danny Inosanto displays the Kris, the national weapon of Java.

An Illustrated History Of Martial Arts In America – 1900 to Present

Israeli-born Isaac Florentine (above, right) is one of Hollywood's only directors to hold a high rank in karate. A Shito-ryu stylist, Florentine had his own dojo in Tel Aviv before moving to Hollywood in 1989. He has worked with the likes of Jean Claude Van Damme, Dolph Lundgren, David Carradine, etc. He has directed dozens of **Power Rangers** episodes and **WMAC Masters**. Among his numerous films are **Savate**, **Special Forces**, **U.S. Seals 2**, and **Undisputed 2**.

James Lew is one of the best-known kung fu practitioners in the United States. A student of Doug Wong, Lew became a nationally ranked kata champion and became famous as one of the top weapons experts in the country. Noted for his flexibility and great kicking skills, he became a popular 'bad guy' in many Hollywood films and later became a top stuntman and fight co-coordinator. Today, he is also into film production.

The 1990s

Maurice Smith was the first American world kickboxing champion to compete in the UFC, where he beat wrestler, Mark Coleman, to take the UFC heavyweight belt. He showed people the value of good standup technique in a mixed martial arts fight.

In 1997, Steven Seagal starred in the film **Fire Down Below** where he plays an Environmental Protection agent fighting a group of big businessmen who are dumping toxic waste in the Kentucky Hills. Seagal, as usual, uses his martial arts skills to overcome his adversaries.   *Courtesy of Warner Brothers*

Frank Shamrock became one of the biggest names in the no holds barred martial arts world, beginning with his first NHB fight in '97. By 1999, he was chosen **Black Belt Magazine**'s Full Contact Fighter of the Year and is considered one of the best fighters.

## An Illustrated History Of Martial Arts In America – 1900 to Present

Adrenal Stress Scenario Training (ASST), in which would be attackers got dressed up in very heavily padded "mugger outfits", was first conceived by Matt Thomas of San Francisco in the early 1970s. Originally called Model Mugging, the program offered everyday women a fast, effective and realistic way to learn self-defense. By the mid-1990s, numerous off shoots of the course were offered throughout the country. Here, Meredith Gold, one of America's leading ASST instructors is shown. Gold runs her own R-A-W-Power program.

A former Okinawa-te black belt, Bridgett Rielly became one of America's greatest female kickboxers, winning world titles in three weight divisions: bantam-weight, feather-weight and super-feather-weight. On February 15, 1988, Rielly won the IFBA Women's World Bantam Weight Boxing title.

In the martial arts comedy **Beverly Hills Ninja** (1997) Chris Farley (left) plays a bumbling Ninja warrior who must prove himself when he is hired by Nicolette Sheridan to spy on her boyfriend. Martial artist Robin Shou (right) co-stars in this funny spoof. *Courtesy of Tri Star*

The 1990s

According to most experts, Rickson Gracie seen here choking an opponent, was the toughest and best fighter of the Gracie Clan. He has been teaching in the United States for over 20 years.

Dottie White is one of the leading female fighters, who has dominated the open karate circuit since 1998. *Courtesy of Larry Carnahan*

By the late 1990s, the demand for accomplished martial arts stunt performers in the movie industry prompted a number of film fighting schools to open both on the East and West Coasts.

An Illustrated History Of Martial Arts In America – 1900 to Present

American martial arts master Duke Moore was the founder of the American Teachers Association of the Martial Arts (ATAMA). Above, a group of top ATAMA senseis pose with Moore. (L-r): Tony Troche, Rick Alameny, Duke Moore, Bernie Weiss, Emil Farkas and Le Roy Rodriguez.

Anthony De Marco, shown winning the 1998 Diamond Nationals, was one of the leading soft style competitors throughout the late 1990s. *Courtesy of Larry Carnahan*

Actor and martial artist Wesley Snipes demonstrates his martial arts skills in **Blade** (1998), where he plays a half-vampire/half-mortal man out to save mankind from evil vampires. The movie had two sequels.

Jimmy Pedro is the most successful judo competitor in the United States. He was on the United States Olympic team in 1992, 1996 and 2000. He was 5 time U.S. National Champion and won bronze medals at the World Judo Championships in 1991 and 1995. In 1999, he became World Judo Champion in the 73kg division. Today, he runs his own judo club "Pedro's Judo Center" in Wakefield, Massachusetts.

## The 1990s

Frank Shamrock (right) vs. Tito Ortiz at UFC 22 in 1999.
*Courtesy of F. Shamrock*

(L-r): Journalist John Corcoran, writer and Taekwondo instructor Keith Yates and Ninjutsu expert Stephen Hayes at the Martial Arts History Museum kick-off banquet in 1999.
*Courtesy of Keith Yates*

Famous Hong Kong actor and director Sammo Hung starred in the CBS T.V. show **Martial Law**, which premiered in September 1998 and ran until May of 2000. In the show, Sammo, who plays a Chinese police inspector working in Los Angeles, shows off his incredible acrobatic fighting skills in every episode, while infusing the action series with oriental philosophy and much humour. *Courtesy of CBS*

**American Samurai** magazine was founded by Bill Bly in 1999. Its primary focus is on the traditional martial arts.
*Courtesy of Bill Bly*

An Illustrated History Of Martial Arts In America – 1900 to Present

By late of the 1990s, 'No holds barred' fighting became the new craze in American martial arts. Due to TVs exposure, these events drew huge crowds and many of the fighters were making big money.

In the 1990s major American martial arts champions such as Joe Lewis, seen here, traveled widely across the United States teaching seminars to students from all styles. Lewis was one of earliest martial arts instructors to begin teaching seminars. Some other instructors widely known for teaching seminars include Bill Wallace, George Dillman, Wally Jay, Danny Inosanto, Benny Urquidez and Fumio Demura.

By the late 1990s, when realistic combat training became wide spread, new equipment such as this Blue Max fully padded safety suit was being widely marketed.

By the late 1990s, some dojos were teaching children as young as 4 to use weapons in preparation for competition.

The 1990s

Christine Bannon-Rodriguez capturing record breaking 3rd gold medal at the WAKO world championships in London, England 1991.

John Su, an extremely versatile kata competitor, is among the top Japanese hard stylists who competes on the open circuit. At times, he will win in soft style division, as well. *Courtesy of Larry Carnahan*

The cane started becoming a popular martial arts weapon during the 1990s when Mark Shuey (the cane master) began to win numerous championships with it. Due to great interest in the weapon, Shuey formed the Cane Masters International Association in 2000 and today travels worldwide teaching practical applications of this useful weapon.

Casey Marks is one of the top kata and weapons competitors in the U.S. She is a hard stylist who has been a champion since the 1990s. *Courtesy of Larry Carnahan*

Deanna Bivins, 3 time world champion and gold medalist at the 2000 World Martial Arts Games in Sydney, Australia. She is also an America In Defense instructor. She is shown here teaching an AID class in Los Angeles.

OFFICIALS L-R: AKIO MINAKAMI, KIYOSHI YAMAZAKI, ROGER JARRETT, CARL HULTIN, DOUG DENNIS, JOHN NANAY. 2ND ROW: CHUZO KOTAKA, BERNARD R. SCARDA, JAMES A. CALDWELL, PAUL GODSHAW, KATSUTAKA TANAKA, KATHERINE THIRY. 3RD ROW: EDMOND OTIS, DEL SAITO, GARY TSUTSUI.

Some leading traditional karate senseis are seen here around the late 1990s. All of these instructors are also top-notch referees at major tournaments.

The 1990s

Kyokushinkai karate champion Tiger Schulman is one of America's most successful senseis, with over 30 schools on the East Coast. He opened his first dojo in the early 1980s and, in July of 1996, he opened his famous "super school" – a 20,000 sq. foot facility in Manhattan.

Stephen Quadros, here with Chuck Norris, is one of the world's leading martial arts and combat sports journalists. He is known as the "fight professor" and is a host and television commentator for some of the largest and most successful fight shows worldwide.

**The Mighty Morphin Power Rangers** first appeared on American T.V. in 1993 and soon martial arts schools around the country were full of children all wanting to become Power Rangers.

By the 1990s, Cynthia Rothrock had become "Queen of the martial arts movies." Beginning her career in 1985 with **Yes, Madam**, she has starred in close to 30 feature films and, is undoubtedly, one of the best-known martial artists in the world.

By the mid-1990s, numerous karate champions like Christine Bannon Rodriguez shown here doubling Alicia Silverstone in the 1997 film, **Batgirl**, were working in Hollywood – mostly in the role of stunt performers. Christine also doubled Hillary Swank in **Karate Kid 4**.   *Courtesy of D. Rodriguez*

# The 2000s

This decade became noted for the phenomenal rise in the business of martial arts. New organizations like the Martial Arts Industry Association (MAIA), which sponsored huge tradeshows in Las Vegas, became widely popular. Black belts were flocking to seminars by experts on marketing, instead of on combat, and dozens of companies were formed trying to educate the dojo owner on how to become a black belt in business. Martial arts business magazines began to be widely read.

Pre-school karate programs were also on the rise, with the four- to five-year-olds now becoming a fair percentage of most dojos.

Full contact mixed martial arts were still growing, with a large television audience and full house for most events.

This decade also saw the rise of franchise karate schools, and multiple school ownership was growing. More and more "super dojos" were opening up and many instructors were now making a "very good" living.

Three of America's best-known martial artists having fun. (L-r) Bill Wallace, Gene LeBell and Chuck Norris. *Courtesy of Gene LeBell*

Written by Jhoon Rhee, a friend and mentor to Bruce Lee, this book was published in 2000 and gives insight to Bruce Lee which has not been in print before.

Four of Hawaii's eldest martial artists (l-r): Jack Wheat, Sig Kufferath, Bing Fai Lau and Jack Holke. All began their training before World War II.

The 2000s

Chuck Liddell (right) and Randy Couture two of America's leading mixed martial arts fighters, battle it out in the octagon.

In the film **Shanghai Noon** (2000) Jackie Chan combines the American Western with Eastern martial arts action. The film co-starred Owen Wilson. In 2003, the sequel, **Shanghai Knights**, was released.   *Courtesy of Touchstone Pictures*

The Shotokan Oshima dojo is one of the most beautiful training halls in the world. Situated in Santa Barbara, California, this 6,000 sq. ft. dojo was built by money collected by members of Shotokan of America. It took over 20 years of fundraising and planning and was opened in August 2000. The sliding wooden doors allow students to work out as if in the open air. Master Oshima lives in a residence near the dojo.   *Courtesy of T. Mazula*

## An Illustrated History Of Martial Arts In America – 1900 to Present

Randy Couture is one of the leading American mixed martial arts champions. A top-notch Greco-Roman wrestler, he won the UFC Heavyweight Championships two times, as well as dropping down and winning the UFC light-heavyweight belt, beating the likes of Tito Ortiz and Chuck Liddell. Couture continued fighting successfully into his 40s and is considered one of the greatest UFC champions.

Tom Callos, a martial artist since 1971, is one of America's top professional consultants to the martial arts industry. His ideas and strategies have had significant impact on American martial arts in the past 15 years. He just launched a new program, the Ultimate Black Belt Test, with environmental perspectives.

Christian Harfouche is the founder of shorite ryu-taijutsu (full-body boxing). A renowned minister and head of the International Christian Karate Association, he was a recipient of the 2004 Global Peace Award for his spiritual contributions to the martial arts.

## The 2000s

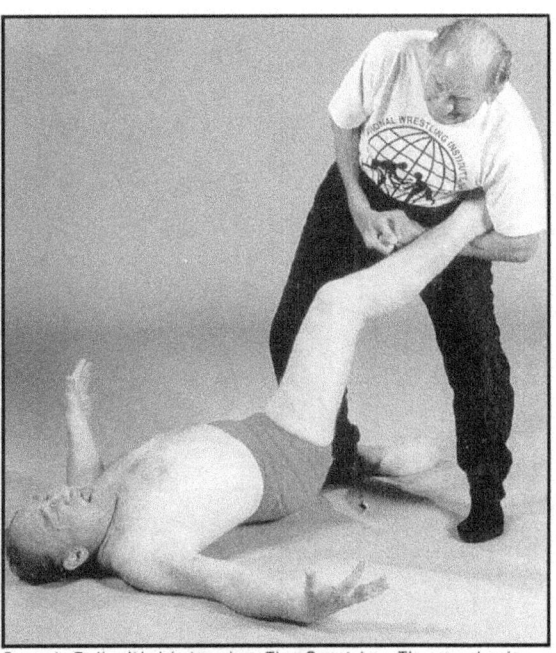

Gene LeBell with his teacher The Great Lou Thesz, who is considered by many to be the greatest wrestling champion of all time. He was trained and managed by another wrestling legend Ed "Strangler" Lewis. Lou passed away on April 28, 2002.

Hock Hochheim, a retired Texas police detective, who holds multiple martial arts black belts, became a well-known reality based self defense instructor in the 2000s.

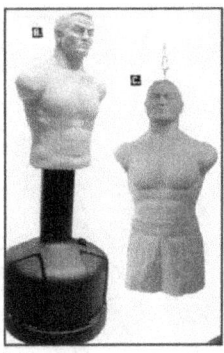

With modern technology, martial arts striking bags began to take on human form.

A group of leading American martial artists gathers at a hall of fame banquet in 2001. Top row, l-r: Bill Ryusaki, Ray Wizard, Bob Wall, Cary Tagawa, Donnie Williams, Cecil Peoples, Don Wilson. Middle row: Howard Jackson, Eric Lee, Blinky Rodrigues, Alan Goldberg, James Lew, Don Rodriguez. Bottom row: Lily Rodrigues, Robert Temple, Art Camacho, Christine Rodriguez and Michael Matsuda. *Courtesy of Bob Wall*

Edna Hima a former top karate competitor is also a Capoeira expert and has gained a big following in the New York area. *Courtesy of Bill Bly*

An Illustrated History Of Martial Arts In America – 1900 to Present

Steven Lopez is the best American Taekwondo competitor in history, winning two Olympic gold medals (2000, 2004) two world championships (2001, 2003) and the Pan American Championships in 1996, 1998, 1999, and 2002.

This book by famous martial arts writer Dr. Webster Doyle was the recipient of the 2000 National Parenting Publications Gold Awards.

Shito-ryu sensei Chuzo Kotaka is a former All-Japan Karate champion. He moved to Hawaii in 1967, and he has produced more American world karate champions than any other sensei in the U.S.

Michael DePasquale Jr., who has been training with his father (standing) since he was five, is a recognized authority on Ju-Jutsu, and street combat. A former editor of Karate International Magazine, today Michael teaches classes in New Jersey when not busy pursuing his interest in the movie business, or conducting seminars on combat Ju-Jutsu. *Courtesy of A. Goldberg*

Tai Chi master William Chen.

## The 2000s

Hideharu Igaki, who came to the U.S. in 1979, became one of the leading sensei's in America. Noted for his fighting skills, he became the kumite coach for the USANKF. *Courtesy of Bill Bly*

Kunio Miyaki is one of the top Shito-ryu instructors in the U.S. A member of the USANKF, he is noted for his kata skill and is often called upon by students for guidance. *Courtesy of Bill Bly*

Del Saito is a highly respected Shito0ryu karate instructor. He has been instrumental in the AAU karate program for years and became national AAU karate executive director in 2000. He teaches in Oregon. *Courtesy of Bill Bly*

An Illustrated History Of Martial Arts In America – 1900 to Present

Texas karate legends Keith Yates (Dallas), George Minshews (Houston) and The Legendary Pat Burleson (Ft. Worth), who was the first National Karate Champion (circa 1964), at a 2000 seminar.

2008 - Northridge, CA
Jimmy James LeBell, grandson of The Toughest Man Alive "Judo" Gene LeBell, is shown here getting in shape to join Stunts Unlimited. In addition to being a legendary martial artist, Gene LeBell is also an accomplished stunt actor in a career spanning over five decades.

George Kotaka (left) and Elisa Au hold their trophies after both won gold medals at the 2002 WKF World Karate Championships. Two years later in 2004, Ms. Au won two more gold medals at the world championships – one in her division and one in the open competition – making her the winningest traditional American karate champion. *Courtesy of Bill Bly*

Shojiro Koyama, a leading JKA black belt, came to the U.S. in 1964 and is the chief instructor of the Arizona Karate Association. He is affiliated with the I.S.K.F under Okazaki sensei. *Courtesy of Bill Bly*

The 2000s

Philadelphia, PA:
Professor Rick Wigginton, 5th from left, a 50 year practitioner of hard core martial arts with a group of his training partners and students in 2007. Professor Wigginton is one of the nation's highest ranked martial arts masters and one of the foremost weapons & tactics trainers. Professor Wigginton has been a professional published author and contributing editor since 1973. Wigginton's articles, commentaries and interviews span seven publishing groups, numerous magazine titles, specials and various newspapers.

By the early 2000s, enough American martial artists were traveling to Japan to train that a book by David Jones, a professor of cultural anthropology and holder of black belts in numerous arts, was a necessity.

Dave(left) and Tim Kovar run one of the most successful chain of karate schools in the US.: The Kovards Satori Academy of Martial Arts, in the Sacramento area. The two brothers have become well known for their innovative marketing and teaching skill and are in demand nation-wide as motivational speakers on the subject of running successful martial arts schools.

In 2001 Hidetaka Nishiyama, president of the American Amateur Karate Federation, was honored by the Emperor and Empress of Japan with the Order of the Sacred Treasure, Gold Rays with Rosette for his worldwide promotion of Japanese culture as a master instructor of traditional karate.

A number of people who have helped the growth of martial arts in the U.S.: Jean-Claude Van Damme (left), Chuck Merriman (right) and Fumio Demura on top. *Courtesy of Bill Bly*

Chanbara, padded weapons fighting, similar to combat with traditional Japanese weapons, started becoming popular in the early 2000s, especially with kids. It was introduced to the U.S. by Dana Abbot (holding sword) who trained in Japan for 14 years.

At the 2002 Battle of Atlanta, Michael De Pasquale (left) and Keith Vitali receive Joe Corley's "Centurion" award. Looking on, from left to right: Glen Keeny, Ben Kikar, Pat Johnson, Ken Ubanks, Bill Wallace, Jeff Smith and Truman Irving. *Courtesy of K. Vitali*

The 2000s

In July 2003, thousands of martial arts fans gathered for the first official Bruce Lee Convention held in Burbank, California.

Famous director Quentin Tarantino's film **Kill Bill** stars Uma Thurman as a woman who uses her martial arts skills to revenge an assassination team, led by Bill (David Carradine) that betrayed her. The film was released in 2003 with a sequel that was released in 2004.

The first Olympic judo competitors who represented the U.S. seen here in their golden years. Left to right: George Harris, Jim Bregman, Yosh Uchida (coach), Paul Maruyama and Ben Nighthorse Campbell.

# An Illustrated History Of Martial Arts In America – 1900 to Present

Two leading American mixed martial arts champions, Chuck Liddell (right) and Tito Ortiz, fight it out at the UFC 47 in April 2004 in Las Vegas. Liddell KO'd Ortiz.  *Courtesy of UFC*

Monica LeBell-Pandis demonstrating a "Love" handle on her father Gene LeBell.

In addition to using her father as an uki, she is also an accomplished martial artist and an FBI agent.

The 2003 film **The Last Samurai**, starring Tom Cruise, gave the American martial arts audiences a realistic glimpse of the samurai fighting arts, as well as the samurai culture of the late 19th century.  *Courtesy of Warner Brothers*

The 2000s

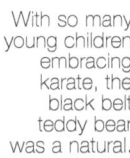

With so many young children embracing karate, the black belt teddy bear was a natural.

The Gracie Museum, located at the Gracie Jiu-Jitsu Academy in Torrance, displays memorabilia of the Gracie heritage that dates back to the early '30s.
*Courtesy of Rorion Gracie*

Cliff Lenderman is one of the most innovative martial artists of the past few years. A student of numerous styles, he now teaches martial arts at his 10,000 square foot facility in Parkland, Washington. Recently, his focus has shifted to the area of fitness and obesity and, to this end, he has developed "Lean and Fit" a program that focuses on a healthy lifestyle. He is also an accomplished actor; Lenderman has starred in numerous films and TV shows. *Courtesy of C. Lenderman*

In 2003, **The New Gladiators** was released on videotape by Rising Sun Productions. This 93 minute documentary on sport karate of the 1970s was financed by Elvis Presley and was lost, until George Wade found it and brought it to Rising Sun, who restored it. The footage features some of the greatest fighters of the time and has original music by Crosby, Stills and Nash.

An Illustrated History Of Martial Arts In America – 1900 to Present

At the 2005 Ocean State Grand Nationals, some of the top NASKA promoters line up with champion, Chuck Norris. From left to right: Christine Bannon-Rodriguez, Don Rodriguez, Manny Reyes, Rick Baptista, Larry Carnahan, Chuck Norris, Joe Corley, Clearmount Poulin, Dennis Brown, John Sharke, Mohammed Jonhash Vash, Ken Eubanks.  *Courtesy of D. Rodriguez*

In July of 2005, Black Belt Magazine hosted its first annual Festival of Martial Arts. The three-day event, held at Universal City, featured dozens of famous martial artists doing seminars, a martial arts film festival, which included panel discussions with industry experts and a Hall of Fame Dinner.

By the 1990s, the American martial arts film has become an excepted genre. This book, published in 2004, examines the history of this specialized area of American films.

The 2000s

Nick Cokinos is a leader in the martial arts business world and is the founder and head of Educational Funding Company, the first tuition and consulting institution in the U.S. A former CEO of Jhoon Rhee's successful Taekwondo school from 1970 to the '80s, he is today the best known managerial expert for commercial educators and has helped some of America's leading senseis become more successful. *Courtesy of N. Cokinos*

This Kung-fu hamster that spins his nunchakus was a big novelty item in stores in the early 2000s.

In 2005, world famous American Judo expert, Gene LeBell, was roasted by the Hollywood community. Bob Wall (at podium) was the master of ceremonies and the who's who of the martial arts world showed up to pay tribute to this living legend. At left, laughing, is Chuck Norris. *Courtesy of B. Wall*

Shotokan Karate Instructor Dawn Barnes was one of the first senseis in the U.S. to specialize in a children's karate program. She is noted for her expertise in the field and owns Karate Kids a chain of highly successful dojos in southern California.

Cathy Cline is one of the highest-ranking female Shotokan practitioners in the US. She is a member of Okazaki sensei's I.S.K.F. *Courtesy of Bill Bly*

Even in the mid-2000s, Ernie Reyes and his demo team were still putting on shows all over the country to cheering audiences. His young protégés were an inspiration to everyone. In the photo is the Reyes family, top (l-r): Ernie Jr., Ernie Sr., and Lee. At bottom: Espirit, Margie, Ki, and Destiny doing the splits. *Courtesy of Ernie Reyes*

Jason Tankson (right) shown delivering an axe kick, is among the best fighters of the mid-2000s. *Courtesy of Larry Carnahan*

# The 2000s

Larry Tattum, one of Ed Parkers' top students, is today one of the world's leading Kenpo instructors. He has his own organization and teaches regularly at his Pasadena dojo.

By 2005, the American Taekwondo Association (ATA) has become the largest martial arts organization in the country, with well over 250,000 members. The photo is at one of the ATA Nationals. *Courtesy of ATA*

Allen Goldberg (right) is the promoter of the Action Martial Arts Magazines Mega Martial Arts Weekend, in Atlantic City, every year (see inset, right). The event, the largest in the country, includes a trade show, an expo and the biggest award banquet in the country. At the 2005 event (l-r): Bob Wall, Bill Wallace, Wesley Snipes and Michael DePasquale. *Courtesy of Bob Wall*

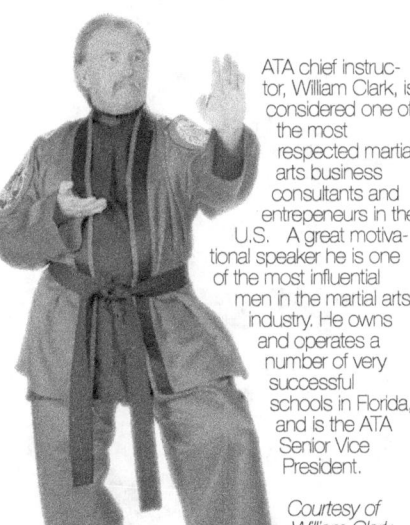

ATA chief instructor, William Clark, is considered one of the most respected martial arts business consultants and entrepeneurs in the U.S. A great motivational speaker he is one of the most influential men in the martial arts industry. He owns and operates a number of very successful schools in Florida, and is the ATA Senior Vice President.

*Courtesy of William Clark*

Mark Canonizado is among the best of the young *Xtreme* forms competitors and weapons champions on the open circuit today.
*Courtesy of Larry Carnahan*

Stephen Oliver, owner of Mike High Karate schools in Denver, is one of the most successful school owners in the country. A top black belt, Oliver is also one of the leading martial arts business experts in the U.S. and is in high demand at seminars and conferences. A formidable speaker and motivator, he is, today, among the leaders of the new martial arts industry boom.

# An Illustrated History Of Martial Arts In America – 1900 to Present

Steve Le Velle, a Florida-based martial arts instructor, is one of the most successful and respected teacher in the arts. Owner of a number of dojos, Le Velle is an innovator and a highly skilled motivational speaker whose goal is to elevate the martial arts industry to top notch professionalism. Le Velle was a former top ranked competitor in forms, fighting and weapons. *Courtesy of Steve Le Velle*

Many of today's top instructors, like Jeff Smith, who run professional dojos, are not only black belts on the mat, but they are black belts in business. *Courtesy of Jeff Smith*

Many new professional dojos divide the viewing area from the workout area, so students' focus is not disturbed. This is one of Jeff Smith's dojos. *Courtesy of Jeff Smith*

Many Americans, who originally trained in Japan, continue to practice and teach the various Japanese Samurai weapons in this country.

Clarence Lee (right), seen here with Leroy Rodriguez, is one of the most renowned Shorin Ryu karate instructors in the U.S. He was the last student of Okinawan master Chosin Chibana, and now teaches karate and kobudo in the San Francisco area.

Gathered in 2006 at the thirty year celebration of the American Karate and Taekwondo Organization are, from left to right: Allen Steen, Keith Yates (a-ka to president) Skipper Mullins and Pat Burleson. *Courtesy of Keith Yates*

The 2000s

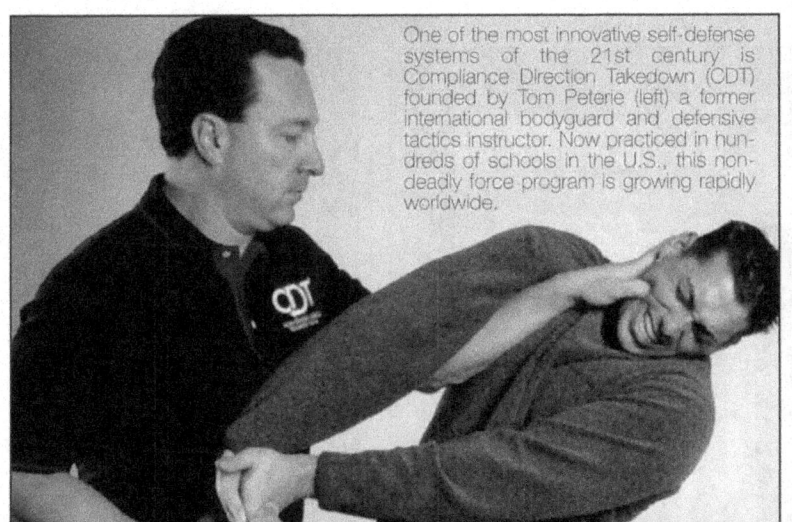

One of the most innovative self-defense systems of the 21st century is Compliance Direction Takedown (CDT) founded by Tom Peterie (left) a former international bodyguard and defensive tactics instructor. Now practiced in hundreds of schools in the U.S., this non-deadly force program is growing rapidly worldwide.

In 2008, martial arts jumped into the 21st century with Dreamworks' release of Kung Fu Panda, a computer animated full length motion picture.

Shaolin Kenpo grandmaster Charles Mattera (right) began his martial arts training in Boston in the early 1960s, and became a protégé of Nick Cerio, with whom he trained for over 25 years. He founded his first United Studios of Self Defense in 1970 and in 1984 he moved west where today he overseas the largest chain of schools in the U.S with over 190 dojos. One of the most respected instructors in America, he was inducted into the Black Belt Hall of Fame in 2004.

In the 2000s, American cable T.V. began to broadcast a number of documentaries on the martial arts. The most extensive series, produced by the History Channel, was **Human Weapon**, which began airing in 2007, and focused on the history and techniques of a different martial art each weak.

# An Illustrated History Of Martial Arts In America – 1900 to Present

Roger Jarret is the owner and chief instructor of USA Martial Arts Training Centers (with over 20 schools). He is one of the most versatile instructors in the country holding black belts in taekwondo, karate, aikido, judo and iaido. He became president of the USA Karate-do Federation in 2006 and is one of the most respected senseis and administrators in the U.S.

Edmond Otis is one of America's leading Shotokan karate senseis. He is the chairman and chief instructor of the American JKA Karate Association, and is the director of martial arts at the University of Riverside, which has one of the nation's largest collegiate martial arts programs.

Frank Silverman, who runs a chain of successful karate schools in Florida, is also the executive director of the Martial Arts Industry Association (MAIA). His goal is to see the martial arts grow and become professional. He is a noted speaker and is highly respected for his business and promotional skills.

Zhang Zi-Yi and Chow Yun Fat (right) starred in the martial arts masterpiece **Crouching Tiger, Hidden Dragon** released in the U.S. in 2000. The film revived interest among many Americans toward the Chinese martial arts. *Courtesy of Sony Pictures*

At the beginning of 2000, large martial arts business-oriented conventions like the Martial Arts Super Show in Las Vegas began to appear. These events often featured dozens of experts giving seminars on how to become better at the business end of the martial arts.

The 2000s

By the mid-2000s, Mixed Martial Arts (MMA) became the new trend with millions of Americans watching the action on T.V.

Anna Burleson, wife of the legendary J. Pat Burleson and the first Texas State Mixed Martial Arts Woman's Champion.

An Illustrated History Of Martial Arts In America – 1900 to Present

Some of the numerous martial arts magazines that have been published in the U.S. since 1950.

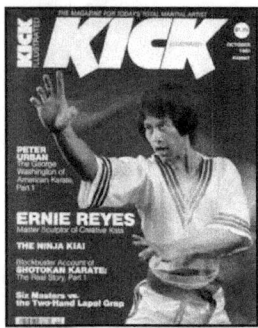   

  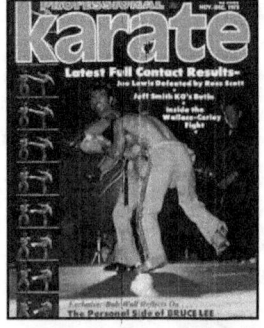 

Magazines

www.ingramcontent.com/pod-product-compliance
Lightning Source LLC
Chambersburg PA
CBHW082113230426
43671CB00015B/2683